Mike McCaffrey, a leading expert on marketing and selling of professional services, lectures extensively and has conducted seminars on these topics for more than 500,000 persons in the United States and Canada over the past fourteen years. He is president of Mike McCaffrey and Associates, a California-based firm specializing in the development and application of marketing and selling concepts in business and the professions. In addition to making frequent appearances on TV, he is a guest lecturer at the UCLA Graduate School of Management and has managed various enterprises, including a PR department for NBC.

Jerry Derloshon is co-author of the *Success Merchants: A Guide to Major Influences and People in the Human Potential Movement* (Prentice-Hall, 1982). He also instructs at California colleges, including Loyola Marymount University.

A SPECTRUM BOOK

Prentice-Hall, Inc., Englewood Cliffs, New Jersey 07632

MIKE McCAFFREY
with Jerry Derloshon

Personal Marketing Strategies

How to Sell Yourself, Your Ideas, and Your Services

Library of Congress Cataloging in Publication Data

McCaffrey, Mike.
    Personal marketing strategies.

    A Spectrum Book.
    Bibliography: p.
    Includes index.
    1. Selling—Psychological aspects. 2. Assertiveness
(Psychology) 3. Success. 4. Persuasion (Psychology)
I. Derloshon, Gerald B. II. Title.
HF5438.8.P75M35 1983   658.8'5   82–16555
ISBN: 0-13-657452-1
ISBN: 0-13-657114-X (pbk.)

ISBN 0-13-657452-1

ISBN 0-13-657114-X {PBK.}

This Spectrum Book is available at a special discount when ordered
in large quantities. Contact Prentice-Hall, Inc., General
Publishing Division, Special Sales, Englewood Cliffs, N.J. 07632.

10 9 8 7 6 5

Printed in the United States of America

Editorial/production supervision
and interior design by Claudia Citarella
Cover design by Judith Kazdym Leeds
Manufacturing buyer: Barbara A. Frick

PRENTICE-HALL INTERNATIONAL, INC., *London*
PRENTICE-HALL OF AUSTRALIA PTY. LIMITED, *Sydney*
PRENTICE-HALL OF CANADA INC., *Toronto*
PRENTICE-HALL OF INDIA PRIVATE LIMITED, *New Delhi*
PRENTICE-HALL OF JAPAN, INC., *Tokyo*
PRENTICE-HALL OF SOUTHEAST ASIA PTE. LTD., *Singapore*
WHITEHALL BOOKS LIMITED, *Wellington, New Zealand*
EDITORA PRENTICE-HALL DO BRAZIL LTDA., *Rio de Janeiro*

To Sharon, Kathleen, Mike, Megan, and Patrick.

Thank you Peggy Stilson, friend and typist,
for your tireless efforts and many contributions.

Contents

THE SELLING GAME:
A TRACK TO RUN ON

4

Entering
the Selling Phase

5

The
Opening

6

The
Interview

7

The
Responding Presentation

8

The
Natural Conclusion

9

Retaining Clients
and Customers

THE MOST IMPORTANT GAME:
YOU 117

10

Setting Your Marketing
and Selling Goals 119

11

The
Self-Image 129

12

Thought Processes, Values,
and Conditioning 137

13

Image Impression
and Affirmations 145

APPENDICES 159

A:
Interviews 161

B:
Questions
and Responses 181

Foreword

My professional goal in life is to get the BS out of the behavioral sciences and make what we know about people come alive for managers, parents, and leaders in all walks of life. That's what *The One Minute Manager* is all about and why it seems to be so helpful to folks in the people-managing aspect of their lives. What Mike McCaffrey, with the help of Jerry Derloshon, has done in his book *Personal Marketing Strategies* is the same thing in terms of how to sell yourself, your ideas, and your services. They have taken the BS out of marketing and selling and made it come alive for all of us as professionals, parents, colleagues, and friends. It has that kind of broad appeal.

A major theme of the book is that success in life is not guaranteed because of your technical skills, education, and experience. They all help, but the key to success is being able to sell yourself, your ideas, and services. The truth of the statement I once heard J. Shelov, a friend and top sales manager, make applies here: "Production minus sales equals scrap." You might have a great product or have a great idea but it remains with you until you have sold it. McCaffrey teaches you what you need to know to do just that.

If I get one or two good ideas out of most books I read, I think my effort has been worth it. There are so many good ideas in this book it is almost overwhelming. Let me just give you a few of my "I learned" statements to share my excitement.

I learned that. . .

- The most important time frame in a speech is the 15-minute period immediately following the presentation.
- You should not expect brochures to generate a lot of business—they only help your image.
- You should spend more time collecting their business cards than giving out yours.
- Published articles in newspapers and magazines are easy to get and are more productive and cheaper than ads.
- Marketing and selling is a process—a flow—there is a beginning, middle, and end.
- People like to help—ask for support and endorsements.
- One of the best ways to develop relationships is to ask advice.
- Selling is honorable.
- Nothing replaces homework.
- The buyer ought to be doing most of the talking.
- You will never be paid a fee or a commission, until you are first paid attention to.
- The single most effective selling tool we have is our ability to ask questions well.
- Brochures, pamphlets, fancy proposals, audio/visual shows, and so forth, don't sell— people do.
- The client is the most important person in any business.
- If you don't believe in yourself—who will?

I'm not going to tell you how well this book is organized (and it is), or how well written it is (and it is), or how clear the examples are (and they are), I'm only going to tell you to read it. It will help make a difference in your life. My wife, Margie, the other Ph.D. in our family, always says "A goal is a dream with a deadline." *Personal Marketing Strategies* can help make those dreams come true.

Kenneth H. Blanchard, Ph.D.
Chairman of the Board
Blanchard Training and Development, Inc.
and
Professor of Leadership and Organizational Behavior
University of Massachusetts, Amherst

Preface

This book is designed to help you market and sell yourself, your ideas, and services more effectively. It is based primarily on my own experiences, and those of my co-author, Jerry Derloshon. We have worked with and known a multitude of people who have successfully marketed and sold whatever talents they have to achieve specific business, career, professional, personal, or social goals. These people include management consultants, salespeople, accountants, architects, authors, entertainers, bankers, advertising executives, management personnel, members of service organizations, and clergy. All have had reason to market and sell themselves, their ideas, or services.

The benefits are clear. These people succeed. They get promoted, they attain more wealth or influence, they become more powerful, they gain more freedom of action and latitude, and they make a greater contribution. What is also clear and paramount to this book is that this success is, in most cases, *not* solely dependent on technical skills, education, knowledge of subject, experience, research, or previous successes. Of course such qualifications are called for. Understanding more thoroughly new dimensions, laws, and concepts can be referred to as technical competence. But again—taking these as a given—what difference does all this make if no one seeks your advice, retains your services, or buys your products?

Are you in high enough demand? Are you getting the kind of recognition you deserve? Do you have the amount of freedom and latitude you want? Can you honestly say you are reaping the kinds and amounts of rewards from your business/practice with which you are happy?

If not, this book will help you.

I have experienced the excitement, challenge, and apprehension of starting two successful businesses/practices—seeing them grow, causing some real wins, enduring some losses, and rebuilding momentum. I have experienced my businesses blossoming and flourishing to the point where I work 180 days a year, live at the beach, enjoy my work enormously and see all of my children's games and extracurricular activities. I ski and surf when I want to, take lots of family vacations, and travel the world with my wife.

I owe this lifestyle (important to me and my values) partially to my technical competence and even *more* to my understanding of the concepts presented in this book. What distinguishes the people who have such qualifications but who are *not* successful from others who have similar qualifications and *are* extremely successful is *marketing* and *selling*!

In other words, qualified people who are ineffective in marketing and selling themselves, their ideas, and services may or may not become successful. There are many who remain anonymous, unrecognized, and unrewarded. Their numbers are legion. The qualified people who are also effective at selling and marketing enhance their chances of succeeding a hundredfold—and these are the great minority in numbers who receive the great majority of rewards!

It is said that 3 percent of the people make things happen, 10 percent know what is happening, and about 87 percent of the people really don't know what's happening. I relate this saying directly to the subject and purpose of this book. Being qualified is a given, or at least it should be so. (Frequently less-qualified people succeed beyond their qualifications because of their ability to market and sell themselves—more about that later.)

There is no substitute for homework, or preparation, or product knowledge, or experience—none. In fact, such learning should be viewed as a process which lasts throughout our careers, indeed our lives. We should be constantly adding to our knowledge, rehoning and refining our skills, and implementing successful marketing and selling techniques.

Many times I have walked our beach and talked with people starting their own business, and *thinking about it*, changing careers, and *thinking about it*, wanting a different or better job, and *thinking about it*. Inevitably, the change or growth comes down to two key elements: competence in your field and your ability to market yourself, your ideas, and your services. I can help you improve your personal and professional lifestyle and gain greater satisfaction and rewards through this book.

This book has three major parts to it. This preface is devoted to the premise that <u>whatever talent you have, whatever service you provide, and whatever ideas you generate must be couched in a business format, ultimately producing a profit—usually money. It is</u> unbelievably easy to get carried away with aesthetics, creativity, thoroughness, righteousness, and missionary zeal because of your own appreciation or the perceived importance of your activity. This too often leads to bad business decisions, which lead to diminished time and resources, which lead to diminished results, which leads to diminished profits.

The first major part of the book, The Marketing Game, is devoted to marketing yourself and your services—how you can get up to bat more often. You can't get hits (sales, promotions, contracts, accounts, clients) if you don't get up to bat. I recommend you carefully study the marketing graph (telescope) and understand the techniques recommended and the philosophies they represent.

The second major part of the book, The Selling Game, is devoted to selling yourself and your services—how to get a hit when you are up to bat—the actual selling presentation of you, your ideas, and your services.

The third major part of the book, The Most Important Game: You, is on self-image psychology as it relates to individuals who have an interest in continued growth and success.

For the purpose of explanation, and logic, the steps presented in the three major parts are structured and sequenced. Obviously these can be flexible and intermixed. Points can be emphasized with greater and lesser degrees and vary with each situation.

Part Three is a completely different approach to marketing and selling yourself, your ideas, and your services than the rest of the book. It may well be the most important part because it deals with attitudes, comfort levels, and our self-image—all essential to our success in whatever we do.

All the skills and techniques in the world will be useless if we are too uncomfortable to use them. The first two parts of the book deal primarily with skills and techniques. Part Three will help you enjoy marketing and selling and become more comfortable with these activities.

A number of Appendices have been provided at the end of the

book. Each is directed at application techniques, that is how a professional who reads the book begins applying the many principles presented.

Appendix A: Interviews   This appendix consists of two interviews with professionals who know and relate to the four phases of marketing and selling and a track to run on. By answering questions these professionals discuss how they themselves apply certain techniques contained in the book. They relate real experiences from different professions. Their perspectives may act as a spring board to others who are interested in modeling approaches that have been proved successful.

Appendix B: Often Asked Questions and Responses   This appendix consists of twenty most often asked questions on marketing and selling yourself, your ideas, your products, and your services. In this section, questions that have most frequently been asked during Mike McCaffrey's live seminars and presentations on the topic are answered. The questions come from a wide cross section of professionals covering a broad range of diverse careers and should be useful to all who are interested in the subject.

Appendix C: Articles   These include reprints of two articles. One written about me and the other written by me. They are included to indicate two successful public image creating activities I have gotten considerable mileage out of.

Appendix D: Sample Letters   This appendix is full of letters that get action. For reference, I've included a number of actual business letters written for specific objectives. All were successful in achieving those objectives. The reader is encouraged to consider similar correspondence in his or her professional practice.

Appendix E: Further Reading: Bibliographical Notes   Here is a suggested reading list of books on marketing and selling for the professional, which I've found particularly useful and informative. Included is a brief statement of each to encourage readers to pursue them as additional sources of information.

Mike McCaffrey

Focus on
The Four Phases of Personal Marketing of Professional Services

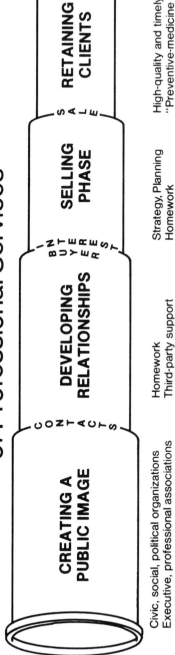

CREATING A PUBLIC IMAGE
CONTACTS

Civic, social, political organizations
Executive, professional associations
Brochures, articles, mailings
Speeches, seminars, etc.
School, church, charity activity
Recreational clubs
Public relations, advertising
Media utilization
Etc.

DEVELOPING RELATIONSHIPS
BUYER INTEREST

Homework
Third-party support
Social engagements
Providing introductions
Offer assistance
Seek advice and counsel
Demonstrate capabilities
Etc.

SELLING PHASE
SALE

Strategy, Planning
Homework
Contacts
Preparation of documents
Selling presentation
Follow-up
Etc.

RETAINING CLIENTS

High-quality and timely service
"Preventive-medicine approach"
Becoming more than business associates
Client retention is marketing
Trouble signs

THE
MARKETING GAME:
HOW TO PLAY IT

Introduction
to Marketing
for the Individual

Marketing in this book is defined as all thoughts, efforts, and materials that result in *buyer interest* in you, your ideas, and/or your services. The emphasis is on a personal or individual approach as opposed to corporate or institutional marketing for an organization.

This book deals with some of the many traditional marketing activities but not with others:

Packaging	Only if you consider dress and appearance as "packaging."
Merchandising	No.
Sales Training	No, except for "training" buyers, clients, and customers to do what you want.
Market Research	Yes, but I refer to it as doing your homework.
Selling	Yes, in great detail.
Advertising and Public Relations	Not in detail, but I give it credit.
Brochures and Printed Matter	Yes, we'll cover it.
Customer/Client Service	Yes, a great deal of coverage.

The reason for including some and excluding others is because *individuals* tend to deal more with the subjects we'll cover while corporate entities and large firms tend to deal with all aspects.

There is a basic philosophy I hold about marketing, and selling for that matter, which directly applies to individuals.

> To increase your business, you need to get to bat more often (create selling opportunities) and you need to get more hits (close more sales).

Most marketing content in this book is written to present ways that you, the *Seller*, can bring the buyer to the point where and when he wants to talk about buying. In a capsule, marketing is designed to get you more selling opportunities, usually eyeball-to-eyeball meetings between you and the client/customer. All thoughts and efforts that precede such a meeting are "marketing," the meeting itself is the selling part.

The *telescope graphic* illustration on page xvii, is a very useful tool to help describe the marketing and selling process. It depicts what I call the "Four Phases of Marketing and Selling." You can easily track buyer/client progression through each of the four phases and monitor your own progress with a potential client or customer.

A real telescope allows the viewer to take in a broad view, and then narrow it down to focus on a specific area. The same is true of the telescope graphic.

The seller of ideas and services requires a large number of marketing "inputs" at the left (wide) end of the telescope in order to retain enduring contacts that eventually become clients and customers.

Thus, there is a system to personal marketing—a flow—from the larger number of potential buyers to the smaller number of actual buyers.

I know many accountants, engineers, lawyers, and sales professionals who use the telescope graphic in their offices to track potential clients/buyers and existing clients/buyers through the Four Phases.

One key point here: You are in a number's game. You need to get to bat often (create many selling opportunities) in order to get a few hits (closed sales). The telescope graphic clearly depicts this process or flow.

Simply stated, the flow proceeds as follows:

Inputs into the telescope (at the right) are called *creating a public image*, which is covered in Chapter 2. The aim is to increase your number of *contacts*. Mere contacts do not always afford you the opportunity to talk business. Instead, at this point, you must nurture and develop each contact into a closer, tighter relationship. So *contacts* lead to a point when you must concentrate on *devel-*

oping relationships, which is the subject of Chapter 3. The aim of developing such relationships is to create *buyer interest*.

At that pivotal point—when another person expresses an interest in you, your services, or your ideas—you enter into the *selling phase*, covered in Part Two of the book, which consists of six chapters.

When conducted properly, the *selling phase* leads to a favorable decision, action, or commitment from the buyer/client.

Having converted a contact into an actual buyer, you need to make an effort to keep or retain his status as a buyer. Thus, *retaining clients*, covered in Chapter 9, is the fourth and final phase in the marketing/selling process. It is depicted as the right or narrow end of the telescope.

Thus the flow, beginning at the larger end of the telescope with lots of inputs, narrows down as it moves to the left—it is an elimination process that leads us to a number of strong and satisfied clients/ customers.

A genuine pitfall for many who are marketing and selling themselves, their ideas, or their services is to correlate their technical competence in their field to marketing.

Wrong again!

Technical competence is one game. Marketing and selling is another. I will assume readers of this book have a high level of competence in their areas of expertise. You must let an extraordinarily high number of people know who you are, what you do, and how well you do it.

Examples?

If you are in the insurance business, you need the names of forty friends of friends, relatives, peers, and associates in order to get ten appointments, which will produce four sales. That's acceptable.

Those are typical numbers for the insurance industry, which has acquired and studied those statistics for more than 100 years.

In baseball, a batter needs about 100 at bats (buyer interest) to get 30–35 hits (sales). And a .300 hitter in baseball is most acceptable.

Cole Porter got "hits" on only 1-2 percent of the songs he wrote. And that's acceptable. Direct mail statistics indicate that a half of one percent is acceptable.

In your discipline, it is necessary to perform or behave at close to 100 percent accuracy—your judgments, performance, and so on. But in marketing, it's different. Lower scores are acceptable.

So begin now to study the marketing telescope (page xvii) as it pertains to your business or occupation. Lastly, remember this point:

> You may be a successful hitter (technically competent at what you do) but if you only get to bat twice in a season, what good is it going to do you?

To determine how often marketers of ideas and services are getting to bat, here is a marketing test that answers these questions:

1. How effectively have you marketed what you have to offer?
2. How effectively have you let your marketplace know who you are, what you do, and how well you do it?

Your professional expertise is not on the line here. This is not a test to measure competence. It is, instead, a test to measure how well you've marketed yourself up until now. If you find a question that is truly not applicable, mark it "NA."

Please get a pencil and take the following test.

THE MARKETING TEST

Assuming potential buyers of your services—clients, customers, good prospects—know who you are and what your services are, rate how *they would perceive you* and your services in the following areas from 1 (low) to 10 (high):

____ 1. Are you in high demand? Is your schedule and workload heavily booked far in advance?

____ 2. Generally, are your fees higher than your competition?

____ 3. Are you perceived as a professional of particularly high quality or unique expertise (graduate school lecturer, Ph.D., consultant to other professionals, author and so on)?

____ 4. Do you have an impressive office location and facilities (prestigious mailing address, high rent area, expensive furniture and decor)?

___ 5. Does your personal lifestyle favorably impress the marketplace and business community (the car you drive, your home, travel frequency, private club memberships, proficiency at golf, tennis and so on)?

___ 6. Have you been awarded honors, selected for appointments or commissions, or cited for outstanding professional accomplishments?

___ 7. Are you associated with prestigious charities, colleges or universities, well-known civic organizations?

___ 8. Is your client list impressive?

___ 9. Do you have a steady stream of new referrals seeking out you and your services?

___ 10. Have you been the subject of a favorable feature article in a magazine or widely circulated newspaper? Have you been interviewed on either radio or TV within the last twelve months?

___ 11. Do you have a positive regional, national, or international reputation in your area of expertise?

___ 12. How does the marketplace rate your overall competence and general effectiveness at what you do?

After rating yourself from 1-10 in each of the categories, add up your total score. If you answered NA (not applicable) ignore the question for the purpose of averaging your score. Take the number of times you did answer (maximum 12) and multiply that number by 10. To compute your percentage score, divide the second number into the first number.

> For instance, if your total score was 89, based on 11 questions answered (one being not applicable—11 × 10 = 110) divide 110 into 89, which gives you 80.1 percent.
>
> What's your score? _____ percent.

I took the test through the eyes of some people whose names you might recognize. I answered each question as I thought these individuals would rate themselves.

> Peter Drucker, the nation's most prominent management consultant   96 percent
>
> Werner Erhard, the founder of est, (Erhard Seminars Training)   94 percent

Dr. Joyce Brothers, author, psychologist, and TV commentator   98 percent

F. Lee Bailey, renowned attorney   96 percent

Earl Nightingale, radio show personality and chairman of Nightingale-Conant Corp.   96 percent

Each of these individuals scored at or near the top with the exception of a few "NA" questions. These people have marketed themselves and their services beautifully. What separates them from millions of other outstanding consultants, seminar leaders, psychologists, attorneys, and "experts" is not necessarily their competence. What distinguishes them is how well they've marketed (and been marketed) themselves. Technical competence is important but frequently not discernible by the layman buyer, and usually not by the masses.

The same principle applies to you.

Being "good" at something and being "marketed" extremely well are two different things.

There are a great many writers in the world. Not all of them get published. There are a great many attorneys in the world. Not all of them get associated with prominent personalities. There are a great many management consultants, architects, accountants, and surgeons but only a few would score in the top percent on the marketing test you just took. If you want success in your field, it will help you to move gradually in several of the twelve areas toward the "10" rating.

1. Be in high demand.
2. Command higher fees than your competitors.
3. Be recognized as having a high degree of expertise.

These are characteristics of the most successful "marketers" of professional services. These are characteristics of winners; of people who have successfully marketed themselves.

Having completed the Marketing Test, the next chapter will present ways in which you can move toward the "10" rating in each area. You will accomplish much of this by "Creating a Public Image."

Creating
a Public Image

Remember the oft-quoted saying, "It's not *what* you know, but *who* you know that counts"? It was true the first time you heard it, and regardless of how you feel it is still true today. Even more precisely, what counts is *who* knows you and *how favorably* they perceive you. Because of the extreme weight and importance of your image (who knows you and how favorably you are perceived), creating a public image is the first phase of marketing and selling yourself, your ideas, and your services.

Your public image can be enhanced or diminished on a golf course, at a restaurant, during a meeting, while you're giving a speech or presentation, or doing charity work. In fact, anything you do in public affects the image you are developing.

And because creating a public image is a necessary antecedent to ultimately "making a sale," we will devote a considerable amount of attention to the subject. One important prefacing remark: It is not always necessary to build a positive public image in your discipline or chosen area of expertise before establishing an image in nonwork related areas. For instance, through active participation in charitable organizations, you may be perceived as a doer, a go-getter, a pleasant and competent individual. This perception may precede someone's knowledge that you are a certified public accountant. But having already "established" yourself in their minds as competent and easy to work with, their perception of you can easily be transferred over into business concerns. I call this the "transfer rule."

The point is simply this: Your image is of utmost importance

in the marketing and selling process. Your image will help you get more contacts and as a result, more opportunities to make the sale.

DETERMINING YOUR PUBLIC IMAGE SOURCES

Three important criteria govern how you generally go about creating and enhancing your public image.

1. Find activities or outlets you enjoy.
2. Be an activist, a doer.
3. Make sure the ground is fertile.

The first criteria, "enjoyment," is vital. You must put yourself in positions and situations that can be thoroughly gratifying to you, giving you satisfaction and a good feeling about how you're spending discretionary time. Only if you enjoy the activities and events in which you place yourself, can you meet the second criteria: Be a doer.

Outlets for "doing" can be found in a wide variety of *civic*, *social*, and even *political* organizations that always need "take charge" individuals, or leaders who get other people to rally behind them. Rotary, Lions, Women's Clubs, Red Cross, United Way, Big Brothers, Muscular Dystrophy and March of Dimes are a few of the many civic and social groups and activities where individuals can help "create" a public image for themselves.

Activism in political organizations is a good source of image building too. Chairing a committee, helping in elections, and speech-making, are all opportunities to let others see you perform. Again, the Transfer Rule is invoked. People tend to judge you to be as competent in your professional undertakings as you appear to be in your extracurricular activities. In addition, church and school related activities—fund raisers, special seminars, and events—have an added quality that many secular involvements don't have. I'm referring to a kind of "bond" that seems present when people pool their efforts and resources together in a great and worthy cause. It is a nonverbal kind of bond you don't normally talk about but deeply feel. In other words, raising $25,000 for a church-sponsored free medical clinic creates a feeling of shared accomplishment.

Your involvement and activism, brings out your leadership qualities. Your willingness to take charge, or pitch in and help, will be recognized by others and appreciated. People are genuinely impressed by the efforts of others. Those same people will remember you when it comes time to buy whatever it is you're selling.

Meeting the first two criteria—doing what you enjoy and being very active in your participation—sets up the opportunity for you to reap sales from your efforts. You make contacts wherever you go, and are constantly adding to or detracting from your public image. Why not commit yourself to (a) enjoyable activities in which you are (b) actively involved that (c) is fertile ground? By fertile, I mean activities, organizations, events, and situations that may possess selling opportunities for you later on.

Here are several "more and less" examples of fertile ground for the marketer of services and ideas.

More Fertile	Less Fertile
Private country club	Local public courts
School board	PTA
Chamber of commerce	Jr. Chamber of Commerce
Big Brothers	Little League
Athletic Club	YMCA Gym
Yacht club	Joe's-Rent-A-Sloop
Friends of the Opera	Tex Smith's Country Western Trio

My point is that you need to work fertile, productive soil. Your discretionary time can be converted to discretionary income if you spend it wisely. Meet the three criteria I've presented and you'll be pleased at the results.

I'm not suggesting you become involved in your church or Big Brothers solely because of your business interests. I am recommending such activities and affiliations only if (a) you want and would like to get involved, and, (b) if you can be active and sincere in what you're doing. You only have so much time. Look for activities that can be emotionally and monetarily rewarding.

If you are highly competent at what you do and proud of your services, goods, or ideas, why not make the most of all your contacts, both business- and nonbusiness-related.

We have largely been addressing the subject of how you spend social time in public creating a public image. Now we will focus on specific vehicles available to you to create or enhance your public image based on your effort which are tied more directly to your particular occupation, chosen career, or area of expertise.

SPEECHES AND SEMINARS

If you have some ability or feel for such presentations I strongly recommend getting yourself some speaking assignments. Speeches and seminars are superb vehicles to create a positive public image. But there are techniques to be utilized in order to get the most mileage out of them. What is the most important time in a one-hour presentation? The opening first few minutes? The very end? The middle? No! *The most important time is the fifteen-minute period immediately following the presentation.*

It is during this time when three or four people come up to say, "That was meaningful," "I enjoyed your presentation," or "Could you elaborate on this point?" This is when you can take advantage of the real purpose of giving a speech in the first place, and that is to make appointments; or in my case, to create additional seminar business or speaking engagements.

True, it is important to deliver valuable information in your presentation. You'll also get exposure, but the real purpose of delivering a presentation is to set up appointments with those who are keenly interested in you, your ideas, and services.

In the last seventeen years, I've made many speeches that gave me only visibility and exposure. I consider those practically a waste of time. What I want most from speeches is more business volume. I partially judge the effectiveness of a speaking engagement by the number of additional "after the speech" appointments or direct business assignments I am able to secure.

There is power and position at the podium. When you're seen as the "presenter," as the "resource," you are viewed as having additional credibility. And the more people who see you in this capacity, and see how prepared and effective you are, the more likely it is that you will gain additional contacts. Remember, creating a public image is a numbers game—the more people who see you increases the possibility of your getting to bat more often.

The goal of giving speeches and seminars is not only to bolster your positive public image, but to create income—"now money," I call it. Many individuals and firms settle for good "PR" but don't cash in on speeches and seminars because they don't know the fifteen-minute technique.

A national accounting firm once gave a series of about 200 seminars that lasted about two hours each. That's 400 expended hours. The seminars were well-presented, topical, and of value—but they generated no known business for the firm. The reason: The presenters did not understand the importance of using the fifteen-minute technique to pursue appointments.

Another important speech and seminar hint: Have an associate or "supporter" in the audience so they can tell others how "wonderful" you are. For example, "This person is the foremost authority in the Western U.S. on the subject. He's terrific." It is most often better to have someone else rave about you than for you to rave about yourself.

Here's how I generate additional business from speeches. It is a given that the speech should be a good one. Good speeches are characterized by a fast pace. Avoid going over an hour to an hour and a quarter. Begin with a catchy, thought provoking idea, a challenge, or a controversial and topical issue full of substance, support it with real-life examples in the middle, and end with an inspirational or helpful upbeat message.

A good speech entertains and educates equally well. Although it is clear that entertainers are paid far better than educators, the reader's audience will generally perceive they want education. And despite the above parameters, the 15-20 minutes following the speech (or seminar) is still the most important time. That is when you have an opportunity to sell yourself, your ideas, and your services. This 15-20 minutes should end with (a) more business on the spot, or (b) an appointment to sell more business, or (c) a legitimate reason for another contact through phone or mail—in that order.

These are some of the encounters you should seek out, and some suggested responses.

A. Someone hears you and wants you to speak or make a presentation to another group—an on-the-spot request for your services.
 1. First, thank them and inquire about the nature of the meeting, who will be there, the location, the meeting's theme, and so on.
 2. Let the inquirer know that the meeting he/she is describing sounds very interesting, challenging, important, or special, and it fits what you have to offer. Then let him/her respond. They will confirm this.
 3. Qualify the inquirer by saying:
    a. You sound serious about my participating (silence)?
    b. Is this something you're certain you want to proceed with?
    c. How sure are you about having me present?
    d. Would you like me to be involved?
    e. How would you like me to be involved?
 4. Get out your calendar or appointment book and confirm the time, date, and location.
 5. Let him bring up question of fee at this point—he may not; you shouldn't. You'll bring it up at contract time.
B. Someone seriously wants to explore things further.
 1. Set a verbal appointment, get his card, and confirm the appointment the next day.
    a. Or do steps 1, 2 and 4 (for the appointment) from (A). Confirm by phone the next day.
 2. Move on. You have what you want. Save the meat for the meeting.
C. Someone is somewhat interested in talking further. This is the lowest level of inquiry, and should be lower on your list of priorities.
 1. Get his/her card. Ask if they can send you something in writing about their firm, project, meeting, and so on, and offer to send something about your services. You've now conditioned him/her for an exchange, so exchange cards. The most important factor here is get the card.
 2. Write a personal letter the next day and send your best printed pieces. (Good luck—it's still not as good as you in person.)
 3. Phone within five or six working days, comment on the materials he/she sent you, and inquire about "exploring what we might do together."
D. Remember, you have a twofold purpose when giving speeches:
 1. Earning your pay by giving them value: education and entertainment. (And yes, you should be paid something—even an honorarium.)
 2. Developing more business through on-the-spot requests, appointments, or legitimate reasons for second contacts.

Getting business from speeches is like a game. If you follow certain successful guidelines you'll achieve what you want. Try the above, they work.

BROCHURES

Brochures are necessary and useful, and I recommend that you have them and use them. People are generally impressed by brochures that have a first class, creative appearance. Photographs or illustrations, effective use of "white space," and titles and headlines are all recommended. The more handsome and expensive looking they are, the better. In many instances, a well presented brochure is your first impression.

Get help in this regard. Either pay to have the brochures done well or get advice from experts along the way.

Brochures suggest credibility and serve as an excellent confirmation of your expertise. While the immediate impact of brochures is tough to measure, the absence of a brochure is most often a negative factor. You may appear small, cheap, or unprofessional—the very opposite of what you want to project.

On the other hand, do not expect brochures to generate a lot of business or create a lot of selling opportunities. That is not their purpose. They are mainly an image-making tool. They can help advance your visibility and exposure, but they will not normally create favorable actions or commitments. They are useful in creating a public image, but they won't do your selling for you.

Also, if you are interested primarily in face-to-face meetings with potential buyers, the last thing you want to do is give out brochures in advance. They either get thrown away, or filed, or worse. By worse, I mean a brochure can actually "satisfy buyer curiosity." The person looks at your brochure, it doesn't "wow" him, so he passes up a one-on-one meeting. The point is that after reading your brochure most buyers will feel they know what you do and how you do it. They don't need to talk to you personally! Oops! Brochures serve as good confirming pieces of material, which further support the buyer's good feelings and perspectives about his eyeball-to-eyeball meeting with you. Remember, you want meetings, not satisfied buyer curiosity.

The only real exception to this principle is geographical or mass marketing. It makes little sense to visit the opposite coast of the U.S. as a result of an inquiry call—send a brochure instead. However, in mass marketing expect a tiny return.

A few words about business cards. Don't give them out too frequently. It is a waste of money because your business cards are often thrown right into the trash can. In marketing, your efforts are directed toward increasing your opportunities to make a sale. Instead of giving out your business cards, collect business cards from other people. Or at the least, exchange cards with others. Having their card is like an invitation to follow-up in an appointment later. Accepting another person's card almost gives you a right to pursue matters further. If another person has your card, you have nothing.

PUBLIC RELATIONS

Relating to the public is what "creating a public image" is all about. This may, or may not be public relations as a formal business relationship with a "PR agency." While everyone is in a position to benefit from maintaining good "public relations," not everyone needs (nor can they afford) formal PR representative. Individuals—accountants, engineers, consultants, advisors, entrepreneurs, agents, mail order people—for the most part conduct their own public relations efforts on an informal basis.

Many can benefit, however, by retaining a PR agency to advance their image. Your decision whether or not to contract with a PR firm might be based on your cash flow. Another old maxim holds true: "It takes money to make money." Often, money spent on direct mailing efforts, display advertising and PR retainers, is money well spent. Individuals in the four "main" professions—law, accounting, engineering, and medicine—seldom undertake such programs under contract, despite quickly eroding ethics codes. More and more, when two or three people join forces, as in a partnership, the "strength in numbers" theory comes into effect and PR becomes more of a necessity than a luxury. Most good PR firms charge a retainer, spell out their goals for the client, and guarantee them results.

Did you know it's possible to trade your services dollar-for-dollar to magazines and periodicals for ads? You invite them to use your services. If you present the publisher or owner with something of value to them and their readers they'll be happy to find space for the ad and maybe even an article. It's up to you to find what they'd like to trade for.

I have similar feelings about conducting direct mail campaigns. Individuals do not often undertake costly direct mailing efforts, for good reason. Unless it is done right the effort will fall flat on its face. Successful direct mailing campaigns feature updated statistical data, demographics, elaborate brochures and mailers, timing, and so on. I contend that if you are paying attention to the personal details of your business, you can hardly be an expert in the sophisticated area of direct mailing. However, your situation may be different. You may have an abundant cash flow and the advice of recognized experts so that direct mailing makes sense. But rather than see marketers and sellers of professional services undertake direct mailing, I would suggest a more personal approach to creating a public image and enhancing your exposure, like the kind we've been talking about.

As far as display advertising goes, most often display ads cannot sufficiently address the marketing needs of the individual professional. It has been my experience that both direct mail and display advertising have little to offer the individual in marketing services, ideas, and himself. Instead, I stress the importance of third party support and the development of personal relationships.

GETTING ARTICLES PUBLISHED

Anytime you can get an article published about you and what you do that is positive and favorable, it is worthwhile, however small the magazine's or newspaper's circulation. A published article about you, your services, or your extracurricular activities (charity, civic, or social) is a third-party endorsement of you. The published article is perceived as having credibility. Many people don't realize how easy it is to have articles published about themselves and their work. The publishers of magazines, trade journals, and newspapers are looking for, and often seeking out, material for articles. The rule of thumb is an old, oft-quoted maxim, "The squeaky wheel gets the grease." If you or a public relations advisor persist with news releases and announcements that have interest and appeal, you're likely to be pleased with the outcome. A degree of creativity will help establish that although the published article will be good for you it will also be good for the magazine's or paper's readers. In other words, attempt to clearly answer this question in all your news releases and publicity announcements: "How does the reader benefit from reading this?" In your handwritten note to the editor present the benefit to the reader. Above all, persist. And whenever appropriate, include a black-and-white photograph with a caption. Your goal is to make the editor's job as easy as possible to run the story—your story.

Another way to gain visibility and exposure through print media is to write articles for publication. If you cannot write these yourself get help from a freelance writer who is experienced in writing and publishing articles, and who also has more contracts than you. A contributed article is offered free to a magazine or newspaper addressing your particular area of expertise. For instance, a tax attorney might offer a magazine a 3,000 word article on claiming charitable deductions. The editorial cost to the magazine is nothing. And the author gets a byline and probably a photograph or two of biographical information. This adds to the author's credibility.

Contributed articles differ from news releases in that news releases are generally *about* you or what you're *doing*, while the contributed article is about *what you know*.

I have benefited from these tools on numerous occasions. Once the piece is published, you may use reprints to sustain the "life" of the article for three to five years. Make copies available to whomever you choose and you can increase this life by having the article reprinted without dates.

OTHER IMAGE MAKERS

Generally, two types of letters can help create a positive public image. One is your personal letter to a prospective buyer or client. The other is the testimonial letter someone has written to thank you for your helpful services to them or their firm.

The first type of "positive image" letter allows you to put your name in front of the buyer or potential client. Normally terse and to the point, these letters "prepare" the other person for an upcoming meeting or, when sent after the meeting takes place, to reinforce key points and establish what the next step is to be.

Your stationery is an important "image maker." Often, as with brochures, first impressions can be made based solely on the appearance of your letterhead. People in various occupations often have quality stationery that projects a positive image to the people with whom they communicate. This help is readily available at no cost from any good local printer. The printer enjoys being creative and offering more than mere printed page. You may do yourself and the printer a favor by asking his advice and recommendations regarding brochures, announcements, business cards, and so on.

CHECKLIST FOR CREATING A PUBLIC IMAGE

Here is a brief summary listing of twenty-one activities and events that will help you create a public image. Check them off one-by-one if you have made an effort in any of these areas.

A. Active Participation in Organizations
   ____ 1. civic
   ____ 2. social
   ____ 3. charitable
   ____ 4. professional
   ____ 5. political
   ____ 6. educational
B. Presentations to Groups
   ____ 7. speeches
   ____ 8. seminars/workshops
   ____ 9. symposiums
C. Printed Material
   ____ 10. brochures
   ____ 11. fliers
   ____ 12. direct mail
D. The Printed Material of Others
   ____ 13. business cards
   ____ 14. brochures
   ____ 15. annual reports
E. Getting Published
   ____ 16. contributed articles
   ____ 17. "ghost" articles
   ____ 18. books by you
   ____ 19. articles about you
F. Appearances
   ____ 20. Television
   ____ 21. Radio

SUMMARY

Whatever you may have achieved as a score on the Marketing Test at the beginning of Chapter One, I encourage you to take the test every six months. Design an action plan that spells out steps you can take toward creating a much broader public image than you have probably considered in the past.

Pay close attention to advancing your image on a broader scale. The more contacts you have, the more opportunities you will have to "sell" yourself, your ideas, and your services.

The next chapter will cover the second phase in the process—relationships. Obviously not everyone who "knows you" from the public image you've been able to create and maintain is going to "buy" from you, so how do you make the most of your contacts? How do you convert contacts into "buyer interest?" You do this by developing relationships with others. The next chapter tells you how.

3

Developing
Relationships

The second phase in the marketing and selling process focuses on developing relationships with contacts, turning even the most casual contacts into business. The goal in developing such relationships is to create buyer interest.

Most selling situations with which I've been involved, were preceded by my creating a public image and then developing relationships. The only thing that has varied from sale to sale is the length of time a buyer has stayed in a particular phase.

For instance, Phase I (creating a public image) has often taken only minutes. A prospective buyer may read about me, see me on videotape, or hear about me from a client—to him I almost instantaneously have become "credible." Phase II (developing relationships) can also be accomplished in minutes over the phone while we chat. Suddenly we're looking at dates that I have available to make a speech or conduct a seminar. The entire sale sometimes is accomplished after only minutes.

On the other hand, I may spend months sending articles and brochures to a contact, trying to establish an identity with him or her. I may spend another several months trying to develop a relationship, and suddenly an entire year has passed without having entered Phase III (the selling phase). Chances are you are in a similar position. But one thing is for certain: Marketing and selling is a process. It is a flow. There is a beginning, middle and end.

The telescope graphic highlights this process. You can track your progress with any given client or buyer through the four phases.

Whatever your strategy to become a better "salesperson," whether you sell intangibles, yachts, living trusts, or exotic products or services, examine it closely. Can you effectively "track" client/buyer movement through the four phases? Do you have a clear picture from where in the marketing and selling process your next sales are coming?

HOW TO DEVELOP RELATIONSHIPS

We will cover seven ways you can develop relationships with contacts or even existing clients and customers so that you can get to bat more often and create more buyer interest in the people with whom you associate. They are:

1. Doing your homework.
2. Gaining third party support.
3. Participating in social engagements
4. Providing introductions and leads.
5. Offering assistance and help.
6. Seeking advice and counsel.
7. Demonstrating your capabilities.

HOMEWORK

Nothing replaces homework, which gives you an understanding about the person to whom you are selling, the products or services involved, and the industry or company. The first step in developing relationships is to do the homework that is required. It will help to know if the other person is a dictatorial type. Or does he espouse "participatory management" or "management by objectives?" Is the other person interested in est, transactional analysis, bridge, or golf. You'll want to know their idiosyncrasies—whether or not they are entrepreneurial, builder-types, or status-quo types.

It helps to know the other person's political and social, even religious, affiliations. Your intent is to know "what kind of person you're dealing with." The reason: Your knowledge will enable you to get close. Getting close is the key to developing relationships.

This sounds like a large amount of research and fact finding. But in fact, doing your homework is not all that overwhelming or time consuming. There is a great deal of information that can be obtained from public sources on practically any individual who represents a potential client or customer. One of the best sources to use is someone who knows the other person's likes, dislikes, areas of expertise, hobbies, and outside interests. The referring source is usually your best source. You may even acquire additional information about an individual from his competitiors.

When I refer to homework I try to underscore the importance of doing homework on an individual—the decision maker whose nod of agreement leads to a commission check in your bank account. You need to know all you can about these individuals. They are the most important people in your working life.

One of the best examples to illustrate this is a story about a fellow who was in Los Angeles. He was joining an exclusive country club in which another office partner was involved. He said to his partner, "I want to meet three people at the next men's function." The arrangement was made. He had his social with the three other people. He hadn't met these three people before. He was introduced and then 4-5 minutes into the conversation said, "What ever happened to that proposed merger between Ajax and Acme? From what I understood; it was signed, sealed, and delivered. What happened?"

This subject, the proposed merger, was in the other person's business. This fellow talked for five minutes and informed, apprised, and educated the man from Los Angeles. Within that process, he became understanding, pleasurable, developed a good business acumen, and so forth as they had an exchange. Then 15 or 20 minutes later he did it with the second fellow. And 15 or 20 minutes later he did it with the third fellow. This man had done his homework on three people and businesses he knew nothing about, and he came away with three likely buyers. He had spent a couple of hours preparing himself. Nothing replaces homework, education, data, and knowledge.

THIRD PARTY SUPPORT

A basic attitude for developing relationships is this: *People like to help.* Psychologically, helping another person leads to a feeling of satisfaction. Being reluctant to ask for help is a common shortcoming among professionals who often don't want to appear as needing help. However, the third party support approach is based on two points, an attitude and a technique. The attitude or feeling on your part needs to be: People like to help you, they enjoy it and are even flattered by it. To the degree you have cultivated this attitude over the years then the following technique will work effectively for you.

1. Help
2. Release
3. Appreciate
4. Make it easy
5. Report
6. Thanks

You *ask* for help, you let them *off the hook* if that's what they want, tell them how much you *appreciate* it and make it *easy* for them to help you. You *report* to them how you are doing and then you *thank them* for their effort—no matter what the outcome.

I have done this a hundred times. I will say, "Jerry, I would really like your help on a certain matter. If you can't do it, or if it is untimely, or if it's a sensitive matter, no problem. But if you can help me I would really appreciate it." At that point Jerry will do almost anything for me. But then, if he agrees to help, I *make it easy.* I do not ask him to do a lot of work. If there is detail work, I do it. If there are contacts that I can make, I make them. If there is letter writing, I write them. Do not ask Jerry to spend his entire life helping. I only want to ask him for an entree—the key thing. The rest is up to me. I *report back* to Jerry about what has transpired. Above all, I thank him for the effort before my success or failure with the project is known.

Here are two ways in which I have used this approach. I know everyone can use this approach, and I know it will make you money. I had a favorable article written about me in a business magazine. I decided to get some mileage out of it, so I had the article reprinted. I acquired the names of 700 top businesses in Orange County,

California. And I said, "Wait a minute!" What I really ought to do is send a cover letter with the article. In the cover letter I ought to have some *third party support.*

I called three people, and I said, "I would like your help on a certain project. If it's highly sensitive or you can't do it, no problem. But I would sure appreciate it if you could help."

Each one said, "Sure what is it?"

"I've got an article I want to send out with a cover letter and I would like a quote from you."

"No problem, sure."

Then I wrote the quote! "Why don't I send you out something, an idea or two. Discard it, rewrite it, modify it, whatever you want," I said.

"Fine!"

That made it easy. I wrote three nice things about myself. I sent them out to three people and they all came back saying, "Sure, go ahead, nice going, good luck, and so forth.

Then I sent out the mailer. Before I sent it out I sent them a copy saying, "Here's how it looks and a special thank you for your effort." I don't want to thank them for helping me get more business. I don't want to thank them for having written anything. I want to thank them for the fact that they helped me. The thanks were not dependent on the success of the project.

I got two things. I got a percentage of 700 businesses who saw that letter. And I also got some "now money." This works every time. It is important that you follow the prescription: Help, release, appreciate, make it easy, report status, and thanks.

Another time my daughter was an honor student in high school but didn't quite qualify for the University of California system. I found a friend who played golf with the highest ranking official in the system. Now, I thought, that was a nice chance for an entree. I said to my friend, "Look, you know that man a little bit and I would like your help on a matter. And if you can't do it, if it's the wrong thing to do, don't do it. But if you can help me, I'd really appreciate it." Then I made it easy. I sent him my daughter's transcripts. I kept him apprised of my daughter's progress. I really didn't have to have him do anything other than put the bug in the chancellor's ear. Then, before the results were in I went to the friend and said, "Look, I want to do something before we even know the outcome, I would like to invite your daughter to come to my Youth

Conference next summer as my guest just because you've been so helpful." He was delighted and most appreciative. I had thanked him before determining the success of the effort. My daughter is about to graduate from a university in that system.

There are dozens of people you have served, and served well. I am convinced they are more than happy to help you. By the way, "who do you know" is *not* making it easy on them.

If you go to your friends and say, "Who do you know that would like to have my services?" that's too hard to weigh. But if you do enough homework and find out that a friend knows eight of the ten people you really want to contact, you can say, "Look, I've got a real quest here. I'm trying to get to (whomever). Can you help me? If it's the wrong thing to do, no problem. I'll do everything that needs to be done in terms of the detail work. I want to make it really easy for you to help me to get to those people." You can bet I'll keep my friend advised of what has transpired and I'll thank him before the results are in. And you know what? He will do it. Don't ask him, "Is there anybody you know?" I'll use that sometimes. I'll do that for example at the end of a seminar when asking for referrals. But you can expect very small percentages compared to pinpointing a target with, "Would you help me with X?"

Another point about third party support: Almost everything is more effective in person. There is the question of time. My business covers the entire country, not just California. So I don't want to go to Phoenix to go through this process every other week.

I honestly believe there are people out there that I have served who like and respect what I do, and would be more than happy to help. If I don't have that, all of this is going to be tough. This is the technique or the vehicle. I wouldn't ask the same person week after week and there are some people whom I would never ask.

If a valued customer/client asks you, "I'd like some help, but if you feel uncomfortable about this, then don't bother." What would you do? How would you feel? You'd help 99 percent of the time. You'd feel happy, even flattered to do so. All I've done, of course, is reverse the situation to make the point.

1. People like to help.
2. They'll do it if you'll help them help you.

SOCIAL ENGAGEMENTS

Social engagements—going to see the local ball team play, going to a golf game, or whatever are very good vehicles for developing relationships. The purpose for tickets to the ballgame is for you and the buyer to get close. You may talk business and you may not talk business. But if the buyer begins to see you as somebody with credibility, warmth, likeability, and so forth you are going to do business anyway. But if you lean on the buyer by talking about business, he will probably be turned off.

For example, two partners in a firm took a client out to play golf. On the 16th hole, while one of the partners lined up a putt, the client jokingly said, "Don't be thinking about all those millions of dollars you are going to receive in the contract." The putter pulled back and said, "I'm not thinking about that at all. What I'm thinking about is the ten dollars I'm going to be taking from you when I sink this putt."

That showed the partner wasn't only interested in consulting fees, taxes, and business. Sometimes that is the most important thing you want to establish in a relationship. The key is to realize that social engagements are *not* designed to promote immediate business contacts, but are primarily a means to create psychological closeness and establish your credibility as a human being. You need to try to build the right atmosphere, and then generate business.

PROVIDING INTRODUCTIONS

Any time I have an opportunity to give one of my clients or my customers a name or a new source that has nothing to do with me, I do it! It enhances my position with the individual. Sometimes I get a phone call and the caller will say, "We want to have you talk on such and such a day," I may not be available. My response often is, "Here are a couple of people I know who are really good on those topics. I'll call them if you are interested." My position with the caller is strengthened. We frequently fail to seize the opportunity to provide leads and referrals to our clients. But in so doing, we get closer to them.

I'm not a great believer in freebee's, but sometimes that's the thing to do. Give them something that they didn't bargain for. See if you can help them for no other reason then telling them, "I'm still hoping to get close to you under the right circumstances. There are no overt strings attached. I just want to be helpful."

SEEK ADVICE

One of the best things you can do to develop relationships is to ask for advice. It obviously makes you appear perceptive. Ask about a subject about which the buyer has some data. Not only that, go back two weeks later and tell him how sound his advice proved to be. What you are attempting to do is to get close to him. And if he can see that you seek his counsel, the likelihood is that he is going to discover you are bright and perceptive. Once again, the transfer rule is invoked. Your capable service in one area will underscore and set the stage for continued or expanded service in other areas.

A common observation particularly about professional firms is that their potential clients do not realize the firm and its members even want more business or are concerned with growth. And the bigger the firm the more this applies. There is an apparent "We're big and successful" attitude, but don't let your response be, "They're big and successful and probably don't need my business." This is true to a great extent because the potential clients have been trained to think this way by the things firm members say. The classic example of this is the answer to the common question. "How's business?"

"We're so busy we don't have time to eat," "We're absolutely buried," "The work load is unbelievable," "I introduced myself to my kids last night," and so forth. Wrong answer, the better one is, "We're really busy but we're also really expanding. We've put on some outstanding new people and we're looking for more business." Let the potential buyer know you're good, and interested in additional business.

A consultant friend of mine recently called on an attorney. After five or six minutes of conversation, my friend said, "You haven't sent us any business lately. Is there something we should be looking at?" They chatted some more and the attorney said he'd think about it. The very next day the attorney called and referred a new client. Clearly a relationship had been established here: a friendly working relationship. If you have such a relationship with someone try the same approach.

DEMONSTRATE YOUR CAPABILITIES

Anytime you have the opportunity to demonstrate your capabilities, you should take it. Here is a different twist: Suppose you find a significant need or want versus an insignificant need or want. From a professional, technical point of view the former calls for immediate treatment and the latter, while legitimate, could be put off for a while. But the buyer is saying "no" to the significant need, and "yes" to the insignificant need. What course of action do you take? Get the buyer to commit to the insignificant need or want.

First, you have an obligation to say, "Mr. Jones, here is the serious problem. Here are the things you ought to be planning for. Here are the things you ought to be preventing."

But if he says, "Yes, I know, but I'm not too interested in that," sell him what it is he will buy! Do this for two reasons: First, it gives you a chance to demonstrate your capabilities. Serve him and serve him well. But the other thing that happens is this: You close out the competition. While you are doing this no one else is going to do this work during the time you are performing this function.

SUMMARY

There are many ways in which you can develop relationships. The purpose for developing relationships is to create buyer interest. By doing your homework, getting third party support, working social engagements, providing introductions, offering assistance, seeking advice, and demonstrating your capabilities you will continue to build and strengthen rapport with the right people.

Do not let any significant amount of time elapse (3-4 months is too much) between contacts with the people and businesses you want to cultivate. Mark your calendar to call, write a note, send an article, have a lunch, and so forth. Stay close and plant seeds for possible business. Plant seeds and stay close so you can harvest.

Out of the many and numerous inputs into the telescope (creating a public image), you will gain a percentage of contacts. From this number, you can hope to focus on the potential buyers of your services. At the point someone expresses interest in you, your idea, product, or service, you leave the marketing phase and enter the selling phase—the subject of the next chapter.

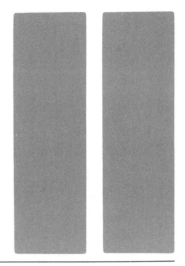

THE
SELLING GAME:
A TRACK TO RUN ON

Entering
the Selling Phase

The selling phase begins when the buyer expresses interest in you, your idea, service, or product. Key to the selling phase is the strategy planning required before the actual face-to-face meeting with the buyer. The title to this chapter could have been, "How Can I Control The Meeting Before it Starts?" What can you do to assure the success of this meeting?

In planning, some of the questions you will want to answer include: Who will attend the meeting, where will it take place, what's the physical layout of the room, who are the decision makers, what are they like, why are they likely or not likely to buy, and what are the problem areas, obstacles, or hindrances? During the selling phase, you set up appointments that are to your advantage, use contacts that are advantageous, do additional homework, make the appropriate contacts, and then prepare your oral and printed presentations. Only after all this preparatory work has been completed is it wise to actually enter into face-to-face meetings with prospective clients or buyers of your services. Once you are at that point, it is essential that you take logical and progressive steps to lead to a favorable action or commitment by the other person.

I have outlined the progression in subsequent chapters entitled, "The Opening," "The Interview," "The Responding Presentation," and "The Natural Conclusion." These steps comprise a "Track to Run On," and it works. But before we review the track in detail, we must build a foundation for the selling phase itself. That foundation is the attitude you need to have when approaching sales activities.

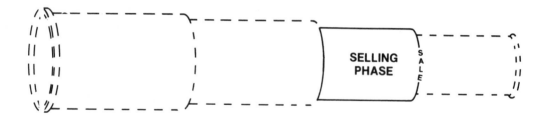

Selling is honorable, essential, catalytic, and causal. You are engaged in it no matter how you label it. Subordinates who "buy" new policies and directions "sold" by supervisors perform better. Children who "buy" guidelines and values from their parents mature easier and better. Spouses who "buy" points of view or personal qualities from their spouses relate better, and, of course, clients and customers who "buy" products and services "sold" by salespeople are satisfied better. A systemized approach to selling is better than a canned one, and better than "winging it." Do you have a system for selling? If not, one will be presented here. Do you have a system for selling that is effective? This one is.

Canned sales presentations are highly criticized and demeaned, many times justifiably so. They lack flexibility, empathy, creativity, and many other qualities. Too many sellers, however, sell spontaneously by the "seat of their pants"—and sell too little as a result. In selling styles, there is a continuum from the canned approach on one end to "winging it" on the other end. Most professionals sell their services and ideas by the seat of their pants. They take the attitude, "I'm good in my particular discipline and because of that, I'll sell easily and often enough." Sorry. It just doesn't work that way. Selling is another ballgame

HOMEWORK

It bears mentioning again: Nothing replaces homework. Just as homework was necessary when you were creating a public image and developing relationships, it is vital as you progress through the selling phase. And it never stops. I am not referring to knowledge of your product, services, or area of expertise. I assume you have that. I am referring to the intelligence information you must gather on the buyer or the prospective client. Doing your homework on an individual tremendously increases your chances for successful selling. Consider how religiously professional sports teams do homework on their competitors. The use of game films is now popular not only in professional baseball, football, and basketball, but also at the junior high school level! Why? Nothing replaces homework. Although game films are not readily available on individuals, you can ask someone who knows the person you intend to meet about that person. When you do, seem interested and curious, not nosy or pushy. You simply cannot have too much information about the client or his company. The more homework you do, the more informed you will be and as a result, the more credible you will appear in the eyes of the buyer. Seek out insiders who can help you understand the decision maker. A better understanding of his preferences, likes and dislikes, hobbies, interests, business acumen, and style, makes you more appropriately responsive to meeting his needs and wants. Your strategy planning— the way you intend to bring about the all-important face-to-face buyer/seller meeting—goes more smoothly after first doing your homework on the individual, or the company. You are better able to determine critical variables that go into planning the meeting such as, where the meeting will take place, who will attend, the subtleties of the situation, how appointments will be made, and what your oral, visual, or printed presentation will be.

YOUR PLACE OR MINE?

The question, "Where do we meet?" is an important one. The three choices are at your office or place of business, the client's or buyer's office or place of business, or at a neutral site. The preferred meeting place from the seller's point of view is most often his own place, provided it is attractive and comfortable. The reason is because the buyer is, to a degree, committed to you and to what you are offering. He or she has already invested the time, effort, and energy to pay you a personal visit. Coming to see you is a kind of endorsement. In that sense, the buyer tends to be oriented to buying, most importantly, from you!

The second reason your place is the best place is control. You control who sits where and the all important room arrangements. You can also control the number of interruptions by unplugging the phone, having your secretary run interference for you, or just making sure everything runs smoothly. This, of course, is especially true for doctors and attorneys. More than 90 percent of the time a person visits a doctor's or attorney's office, the "sale" is made on the spot. These professionals need only to confirm the buyer's intuition that they can help solve the problem.

More commonly, you will meet in the buyer's office. You might be required to if the person is going to see you at all. Some buyers actually don't feel comfortable out of the close and familiar territory of their own offices. Consider the buyer's point of view. He is used to making decisions in his office, there are reports at his fingertips, he can work you in between appointments if he has to, and if he doesn't like you or what you're offering, he can throw you out on your ear. The buyer's office at times is also a "show place" where he is surrounded by memorabilia, records of accomplishments, and certificates of achievements. For many people, the office is a home away from home. If you meet strong resistance to meeting at your place, understand the buyer's point of view and be more than willing to meet at his office. Often, an appropriately placed compliment about furnishings in the office, mementos, pictures, or decorator items is genuinely received and can set a positive tone for the meeting. But keep it short. Being too effusive is transparent, time wasting and boring. Neutral sites are generally good for preliminary sales activities—getting closer, understanding one another, developing relationships and gathering information. I'm referring to country clubs, restaurants, lounges, and so forth. But such neutral (non-business) sites do not work well as backdrops for heavy sales meetings. There are simply too many distractions and too many "outs" for the buyer. Consider such neutral sites good for building and strengthening rapport, and talking somewhat about the product or service. If the buyer wants to get into heavy business talk and specific negotiations, go with him. But let him take that track.

APPOINTMENTS

Having determined the best place for the meeting to take place, the next step in the selling phase is setting up the necessary appointment. Again, this is not a "shoot from the hip" proposition. The question, "Who should attend the meeting?" is of utmost importance. Approaching the issue haphazardly, you might waste a significant amount of time impressing the wrong person and having to come back again for another round of presentations. You either want the decision maker present, or you want the meeting to lead to the decision maker. When selling ideas and services, the more intimate the appointment, the better your chances of success.

Getting close to other people in the organization you are interested in is well worth the effort. Your friendly manner, smile, and pleasant appearance and professional deportment will all help get you the appointments you need. Build contacts. Remember names and who works for whom. All of this is helpful.

In setting up appointments, other considerations include the seating arrangements, what "tools" will be shown or demonstrated if any, and what you'll leave behind, if anything.

Before the selling meeting, you will want to have *your objective clearly outlined* in your mind. Are you looking for a verbal or signed agreement? What would be a "winning situation" in your eyes? What is it going to take for you to win? The objective of the meeting dictates how you act, and your homework will help make the meeting seem as natural as possible—unforced, spontaneous, and sincere. Always know what you want coming out of the meeting. A second choice is worthwhile too.

Also part of the strategy planning during the selling phase is preparation of your oral presentation and printed matter. Although your emphasis should be on the person with whom you're dealing, you do not want to appear ill-prepared or as having overlooked printed documents all together. And here's a key point: The preparation of your oral presentation should precede preparation of your written documents. Determine first what it is you want to say and base supporting materials around your script.

The actual selling presentation itself—the track to run on— will be covered in upcoming chapters. But before we proceed on to the track, it is appropriate to discuss why the system itself is so important to successful selling.

THE TRACK

The track has four major steps. There is a very specific purpose for each one of the major steps. First is *the opening.* The purpose of an opening is to establish value: the value in you, the moment, and in the topic. The second step is *the interview.* The purpose of the interview is to establish a need or a want on the part of the buyer, to get it discussed and thoroughly elaborated. The third step is *the responding presentation.* It is a *response* to a *need* or a *want* that has surfaced during the interviewing portion. The fourth step is *the natural conclusion.* It can also be called the close, or the *mutual* conclusion. Its purpose is to draw a favorable action or a commitment from the other person.

I often describe the track with a medical analogy. Let's say you come into the doctor's office and say, "Doctor, I have a pain in my side." If the doctor were to say, "All right, let's go operate on that side," it would be frightening. You'd run away. But doctors don't do that. Instead the doctor says, "Well, let me get some information here. How old are you? Have you been doing any unusual exercises lately? Have you been eating any unusual kinds of food?" and so forth. In the medical profession, this question-asking process is part of a diagnosis.

A similar diagnosis is an important factor whenever you're selling yourself, your ideas, and your services. I call it, the interview. After a diagnosis is taken, there is a prescription offered, or a course of action. Then, generally speaking, nine out of ten times, there is probably the physician's advice. The same scenario can happen in an hour's time with someone you have never met before with you as "doctor," the buyer as "patient," and your service as the "prescription."

There is one significant difference—patients go to doctors. They say, "I have a problem, help me." I'm going to assume there are not a whole lot of people coming to you or your business, saying, "I have a problem, help me." But this doctor/patient analogy really applies in most lines of work. Accountants, engineers, bankers, consultants, and so forth can all develop "patient" client/customers in an hour's time.

It is interesting to note what happens when you apply the track to run on analogy to various groups. Stockbrokers frequently have a strong opening. They don't waste time with an interview or diagnosis. The responding presentation is virtually nothing because it's frequently almost wholly contained in the opening. They go from an opening right for the jugular vein and close.

I learned that most professional people, and by professional people, I mean anybody who has a given discipline which is not primarily from sales and marketing. I'm referring for example, to architects, or an attorney, or perhaps accountants. They have a given discipline. Along with that there is a need to ask, "Who will listen to what I have to say?"

The reason you are going to be successful or a failure as a management consultant or whatever you do, is not because of what you know as a management consultant. It will depend on your ability to get people to listen to what you have to say. Failure to recognize this is a mistake that most professional people make. They say, "I have this bag of tricks. I know all these good things. I have this vast wealth of experience and knowledge in the field." But if nobody knows about it, it doesn't mean a thing. And there are lots of good people out there who know lots of good things about their discipline. But selling their discipline effectively is another ballgame.

For example, there are many good courses and books that say, "Here are ways in which to present your product. Here are movies, tapes, clever brochures, flip charts, and so on." There are also courses that say here are thirteen ways in which to close a sale.

For most professions, however, the primary emphasis should be on the interview. The interview is where you ought to spend most of your time. And secondly, *the buyer ought to be doing most of the talking*. I'm convinced most professional people miss this important point and do most of the talking themselves; they talk too much about their own firm, capabilities, and so on. The benefits of the buyer doing most of the talking are clear. One, he dictates what your presentation ought to be. Buyers will literally tell you what it is they will buy. Secondly, it makes closing easy. A natural conclusion becomes part of the whole system of getting commitments.

THE EMOTIONAL PEAK

There is a mistaken tendency among some people to press for a buildup that climbs to the close. The natural conclusion, or close, is frequently a big deal; frequently it is an emotional deal. *It shouldn't be at all!* The high point should be at the interview. That's when emotions should be at a pitch. If that happens, everything else is a downhill run. Consider this baseball analogy. If you go up to bat, get a hit, and touch all the bases scoring is easy. However, if you don't get a hit, fail to touch all the bases or even fail to go to bat scoring is impossible. Closing is so difficult because people do not do these sequential things. However, if you do these things first, and well, a natural conclusion is the easiest part. The secret to closing is touching all the bases before you get to the close. Closing should be a result or an outflow, it is a mutual, natural course of action that both parties take.

In the selling phase, you'll also want to pay attention to ways in which you can make it easy for the buyer to buy. Often sellers make it unnecessarily difficult for buyers. For example, I had a positive contact with a very large distributor of audio cassette tapes. We had constructive conversations and were mutually interested in working together but had not yet figured how to do this. The distributor specialized in audio tapes to the man on the street for self-learning and for a selling price around $40. I had a product he liked but it was on video tape, sold to corporate executives for training for middle- and lower-level management people and carried a selling price of $450. As the seller I needed some way to make it easier for the buyer to buy.

I decided to take the audio portion from the video tape series, put it into audio cassette form, mocked up an audio cassette album, put the new audio cassettes in the album, mocked up a brochure that promoted the audio cassette album and presented this package to the distributor. He responded by giving me a check on the spot. I had been asking the buyer to change to a new customer, to a new product, and at a new price. By adapting my product to his product, his customer, and his price I made it easy for the buyer to buy.

Another instance of this is when I have a speaking engagement in Cleveland with expenses paid, it makes sense to contact other clients or potential buyers in the area and attempt to interest them in buying my services for fees only because the expenses have already been contracted for the first buyer (or you may opt to offer expense splitting to both buyers). Buyers like what they perceive to be "deals" and they like the thoughtfulness this represents.

It is a good practice to notify your clientele, customers, or would-be buyers of your upcoming trip, program on a certain city, or a service you are providing for one person or firm that might be applicable to another.

SUMMARY

The selling phase of marketing and selling yourself, your services, and ideas should have a flow to it. Think of the preparation that goes into getting into the selling situation itself. We've discussed creating a public image to get more contacts and developing relationships—to get more opportunities to get to bat. Entering the Selling Phase, you do more homework, plan your strategy, make appointments, use your contacts, prepare your oral presentation and written documents. The next four chapters of the book are devoted entirely to the selling presentation—the track—what you do now that you're at bat.

5

The
Opening

You've seen it a hundred times: a car nearly out of control comes around the corner and screeches to a halt. A man leaps out, gun in hand, with a crazed look in his eyes. People within a five mile radius either run for their lives or lie face down on the ground in absolute fear of death. The gunman runs for the nearest brick wall. Hot on his heels is the star of the cop show—square jaw, determined look in his eyes, tight lipped. He raises his pistol and points at the fleeting figure, and yells, "Stop or I'll shoot."

The gunman spins around and points his .45 caliber weapon at the policeman, poised to fire.

What happens? You want to know don't you?

What often happens is a cut to the title of the show or credits. You're left sitting with a pounding heart, moist palms, and short breaths. You've been hooked by a *good opening*. I hesitate somewhat to use the TV analogy, but clearly the opening/hook is a tried and true principle in selling. Something needs to happen within the first three to five minutes with the buyer that interests him in you and what you have to say or offer. To miss this point is a serious mistake. If you do not accomplish this within five minutes, the rest of the selling process—the interview, responding presentation, and conclusion/agreement will be an uphill battle.

I recommend you go into every selling or persuading situation with the understanding that *every situation is unique*. Be thinking to yourself prior to the opening:

This man or woman is different.
Their situation is unique to them.

This guy is special for XXX reason.
There's more here than meets the eye.

For so many professionals who sell, the people to whom they are selling have often, in the course of a single day, already experienced numerous selling situations. You're not always the first person to get to the buyer. For that reason, you must be different from the others in some valuable way regarding you and what you offer. The word "valuable" was chosen very carefully.

Value is something you need to establish in every selling situation. And having established it, you must maintain it.

People pay attention to any sensory input in direct relation to the value they perceive in a particular source. People pay attention to other people in direct relation to the value they perceive in the other person. You are paying attention to this book in direct relation to the value you perceive in it. Not because I am saying such and such is important, or "it works," but instead, you perceive value in it for you—entertainment, information, a few useful ideas, or a banquet of practical techniques. Remember, you will never be paid a fee or a commission, until you are first paid attention. Therefore, it is imperative in selling to establish value in you, the moment, or the topic very quickly. This is the purpose of what I call "the opening." It is only after having established value can you realistically expect to effectively negotiate a favorable commitment or action from another person. If you don't you will be perceived by them as "value less."

There are two important ways to establish value at the beginning of a selling presentation. First, through your presence. And secondly, through your opening statement. Often, the issue of appearance and physical "packaging" is overstressed. I do not suggest that everybody who wants to sell anything has to go out and buy a $500 suit, a $150 pair of leather loafers, a $200 leather briefcase, and a gold bracelet. Being overdressed or being dressed inappropriately for the situation is as bad as being downright sloppy.

I strongly recommend that people should dress on the "business-conservative" side. If you are professional in your work, I assume your appearance is neat, well-groomed, and clean. Additionally, you want to appear tastefully accomplished and successful, perhaps almost entrepreneurial.

Imagine sitting in your office at your desk, reading, writing, or making a phone call when someone appears at your doorway asking to speak to you. You have not met this person before. At first glance, you see the person is of average height and build, has a very pleasant smile and well-dressed appearance. The person has one opportunity to make a first visual impression on you and the process has already begun.

The same is true for you in any selling situation. The buyer is judging you, your appearance, and your demeanor. People want to buy from "successful" purveyors of services and ideas, not from people whose appearance triggers a negative reaction or feeling.

But let's consider your presence in more detail. By presence I refer to *how you look and how you act*. Your eye contact, handshake, how straight you sit or stand, and all the nonverbal ways you send messages to others are included.

We've all been admonished not to judge a book by its cover and yet we do it everyday. A conservative estimate would place the number of books sold solely on the cover in the millions. It is staggering to think how often we "sell" or are denied the opportunity of "selling" on a similarly quick and very superficial and unfair judgment. But we are.

> Help make it easy for you and the buyer to get close by showing him/ her your best you—don't make waves by appearing inappropriate.

John Malloy's book, *Dress for Success* (see Bibliographical Notes) is the best single source regarding appropriate dress and appearance for the business environment. I recommend it highly. Malloy is not a fashion designer intent on selling clothes. He is an experimenter with what clothes "work" in the business setting and what clothes don't work. Malloy's main theme is that dress should be the "business-conservative" side with some exceptions due mainly to geographical differences. The point is: Don't discount the potential benefits—and detriments —of your appearance.

The only acceptable personal packaging consideration is to dress the way you think the buyer thinks you ought to dress. There are people who are uncomfortable sitting next to someone wearing a three-piece suit. And there are people who feel uncomfortable sitting next to someone who is wearing a white T-shirt with holes in it. If you can make the buyer comfortable with, and even attracted to, your dress or appearance, you are beginning to win.

Another important factor is how you position yourself physically in the room with the buyer. I favor physical closeness, which I tend to believe helps create psychological closeness. The attitude you're trying to create is: "It's you and me, buyer, against the problem. Together we'll find a solution." It's not you versus the buyer. It's you *and* the buyer versus the problem!

Office arrangements are often overlooked in marketing and selling considerations. Look at the diagrams below.

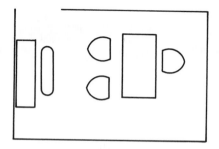

Rather traditional. Notice how the desk serves as a kind of barrier between the office guests and the occupant. A dividing line is suggested that puts you (the seller) on one side and the buyer on the other. A slight change in the diagram renders the dividing line, and the desk/barricade obsolete.

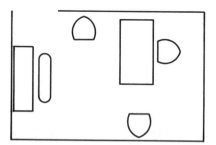

Almost any time you have the opportunity to sit close to the buyer you should do so because you have a better chance of establishing psychological closeness. This point isn't gospel—there are no "absolutes" when it comes to selling techniques. Sometimes office chairs are so heavy you'd strain yourself trying to move them, and of course the buyer darn well doesn't want you rearranging his or her furniture. But often, you *can* subtly move a chair and slide a little closer—appearing enthusiastic, energetic, interested, and so on. Getting close can be the key to getting psychologically close. To accomplish this, you might have a tool, proposal, or instrument in your hands that you'd like to review with the buyer. "I'd like to point a couple of things out to you regarding (whatever it is in your hands)." This requires that either you move alongside the buyer or he moves alongside you.

Here is the worst office arrangement I've ever faced in a marketing or selling situation.

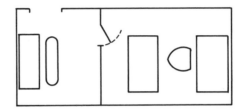

I came into the room, sat down, and had to wait for the buyer to turn around. I talked not only over the man's desk but over a wall from a certain distance! The guy was saying, "Don't get close to me. Don't even try." I recognized there was no way I could win so I decided to get fascinated with the products his company manufactured. I asked the man to give me a tour through the plant and soon, he was introducing me to a lot of people, and calling me "Mike." After the tour, he invited me in (beyond the "great wall"). Recognize though, that some people are uncomfortable with closeness of any kind and you'll do better to appreciate their space, respect their position, and deal with them as best you can.

Board and conference rooms present some interesting opportunities as demonstrated by the diagram below.

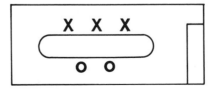

This is a negative situation, What you want to accomplish is to gather around the table as "friends" as depicted in this diagram.

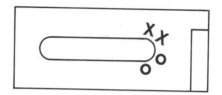

You can bring the latter arrangement about sometimes by merely requesting that seating arrangement, or by getting there early and setting things on the table, indicating to the others where they are to sit. A little assertiveness on your part is required here.

Prior knowledge about meetings is most helpful. I once received a call from an attorney, and through the call I learned some valuable information I think contributed to my ultimately successfull selling presentation. I learned there would be three or four attorneys in addition to the one who called me to set up the meeting. I decided to arrive fifteen minutes before the start of the meeting. I moved chairs around, jockeyed positions, and established "control by precedence." I am a great believer in control. I always try to establish it, and when I get it I try to keep it in every marketing and selling situation.

It is appropriate to mention a few considerations about non-verbal communications, or "body language." You do certain things that fairly accurately indicate your mood at a particular time. Buyers do the same kinds of things, tipping off what they are "feeling." Accept these items as indicators and be responsive when you see them. Folded arms across the chest reflects defensiveness and unwillingness. You might penetrate this by requiring the buyer to hold something you've given him or her. Unfolding their arms may actually diminish their defensive posture. Aggression is often suggested by the "hands-on-hips" position—ready for the fast draw. It is a "tough guy" kind of posture that John Wayne often took. Putting something in the hands often diminishes the "them versus us" attitude and builds more of a "we" attitude.

Although I do not intend to spend much time addressing body language, I want to give the subject credit. You can often "read" another person, or at least get a fair idea of their attitude at a given time. There are several good books on the subject, including *How to Read a Person Like a Book*, by Calero and Nierenberg; and *Body Language* by Julius Fast (see Bibliography).

Another factor to consider is what you carry into the buyer's office. A small, unobtrusive leather or vinyl carrying case, approximately twelve by sixteen inches is the most I would recommend. More than that makes you appear armed with weaponry. Sometimes with two or three pieces you appear as though you have a whole arsenal.

Many years ago when I was "cold calling," the following factors were present. I was on straight sales commission, selling a long weekend seminar for husbands and wives, and the topic was self-image psychology. It cost $600. We had no real track record because we had only been in business for one year. I made $100 if I was successful. In the beginning, I wasn't successful and things were really tight. I would find an industrial area, park my car, and go about knocking on doors and asking for the president or general manager. I carried with me only sheets of paper in my vest pockets to appear unarmed and safe. Each sheet contained people who had attended our program and who were associated with a particular industry—finance, manufacturing, consumer sales, and so on. The only weapon I ever pulled out was the sheet with the people I though the president or general manager would know and relate to. This still carries over to the selling I do today. The less "armor" the easier it is to develop psychological closeness.

During your opening statement, your appearance, the way you "carry" yourself, and how you arrange seating in the meeting all tend to make the interviewing and presenting steps easier. Do whatever you can to bring about "closeness," and create as many positive signals as you can.

Recalling the phases and steps we've already discussed, you've arrived at the buyer's home base. You've done your homework, your appearance is neat and appropriate. You're led to the office where the buyer is waiting. Your appearance, handshake, smile, and so forth are all working for you. You're able to position yourself in the room to diminish any "barriers." This is the critical time—the time that says, "Now let's talk about what we're here to talk about." You have the buyer's attention. Your opening statement should establish value in yourself, the moment, or the topic within three to five sentences or you're making things difficult for yourself.

After you deliver your opening statement, you want the other person to feel pleased that they took the time to see you. There are three types of opening statements that serve to do this.

1. Curiosity-peaking statement
2. Benefit statement
3. Warning statement

Or you can combine the three for added effect.

One of the best opening statements I've ever heard came from somebody in the tax consulting field, which has built in interest to anyone who pays taxes—which is just about everyone.

It went something like this: "Mr. Jones, as you know the legislature has just enacted Law ABC. And we know the result of the passage of that legislation is going to have the following impact on your industry (and the consultant gave the other person a verbal blow to the head). We also know the legislation is going to cause this. However, we at XYZ Tax Consultants prepared for the passage of the legislation and have concluded certain firms in the industry will be advantaged tax-wise like they have never been before and I think your company is one of those."

1. Pique curiosity
2. Offer a benefit
3. Give a warning

Not a bad opening statement indeed. It's quite like a doctor saying, "I think you're going to die the way things are going but I might be able to save you."

When done well, effective opening statements require the buyer to think, "My God, go on tell me more. You're valuable. Please stick around for a while. I need you!" These types of (rather dramatic) opening statements are useful when you're meeting potential clients or customers for the first time. Once you're seeded with an individual or firm, they are not as necessary or appropriate. The opening statement also works well on the phone to secure in-person appointments at a later time.

In your business or occupation, you need to have opening statements that do something to people. They must make them think you are different, special, better, and apart from the rest of the world, an expert, an authority, or the person with "the answer." An effective opening statement satisfies the purpose of the opening as the first step in the selling process. It establishes value in you, the moment, or the topic.

You are the best author of opening statements you can use in your business or area of expertise. But here are a few that will give you some idea of really effective opening statements.

1. Mr. Johnson, in preparing for this meeting we've learned your firm is spending a substantial amount of money on training for your people. For twelve years we have specialized in analyzing the effectiveness of training programs. Our experience has shown without exception that certain training programs are more effective, accomplish their goals, and are cost effective, and that some training programs simply are not. Further, our experience shows it is frequently possible to spend less dollars than you may currently be spending and receive even better training (here we've tried to establish credibility and pique his curiosity regarding the possibility of more for less).

2. Mr. Green, the Acme Corp. has successfully established itself in two ways: (1) the unique clientele with which you deal, and (2) the uncommon service you perform. Yours is the kind of business we like to work for because we too feel in our own discipline we have a most unique clientele and uncommon service. I think we fit well, and the match is good, and I'm here to demonstrate just how I think we can help each other. (Here we've attempted to identify with our mutual disparities.)

3. When the buyer refers favorably to earlier work you performed with a referring source, seize the opportunity to say, "Yes, we enjoyed that project. What did George tell you about it?" (Better the buyer should give the opening statement than you. If he is willing to extol your virtues, make is easy for him.)

4. Mr. Smith, we have consistently earned over 16 percent on return for our clients. We provide this service for E.F. Howton, Prize Watershed, Connecticut Specified Life Insurance, and House Savings and Loan. My purpose in talking with you is to explore if and how we might provide you with the same service and the same return (name dropping).

The best opening statements usually come from having done your homework well so that you can touch a nerve or a hot button. The next best opening is one that is carefully structured to appeal to buyers and can be used several different ways with modification.

Let's assume you can sense your opening was a good one. The facial expression or his/her verbal expression tell you so. They are now saying "go on." Don't!

This requires self-discipline. But don't spill the beans now. One of the easiest things you can do is hint at a solution in your opening and then reveal your whole hand prematurely. This is a mistake. Take them into an interview. You've thrown out the bait and they are nibbling. Now set the hook with a good interview on his needs, wants, concerns, goals, and so on.

SUMMARY

Openings are best when they either (a) pique curiosity, (b) provide a benefit, (c) warn of danger, or (d) all three. You will never be paid a fee or a commission until you are first paid attention.

Through an effective opening, you'll establish value in yourself, the moment, or the topic—whatever it is you're trying to sell. Personal appearance is important—I don't belabor the point. But it needs to be mentioned. Like openings, you only get one chance to make a good first impression. Psychological closeness is something I place a great deal of importance on. Especially during openings and subsequent steps in the track to run on. Your body language is as important as your appearance. Recognize this fact in yourself and in others. If your opening is excellent—you've piqued curiosity, explained a benefit, or warned of danger—and the other person is definitely with you, you might feel inclined to go right into a selling or responding presentation. Don't do it! Take them into the interview, the subject of the next chapter.

The
Interview

During the opening phase of your selling presentation as we discussed in the previous chapter, you opened a communications channel between yourself and your prospective client. The interview follows next. The interview will occupy most of the time you spend face-to-face with a prospective buyer, and the buyer should do most of the talking. This is the most critical phase we will discuss.

One of the most common faults among people who sell is a tendency to avoid doing the necessary work a successful interview requires. Instead, most try to dazzle the potential client with footwork by expounding on all the wonderful things they and their firm have done for others.

Your prospective client really couldn't care less. He wants help and you've got to demonstrate that you're the one who can help him. So the first order of priority is your diagnosis of the client's situation and his needs. Only when an effective diagnosis is complete can the professional present his strengths. And, not surprisingly, these strengths can perfectly match the potential buyer's needs or wants.

A doctor/patient relationship is an excellent analogy to consider with respect to the interview. The physician spends most of his time examining the patient—taking x-rays, blood pressure and other readings. He also does something very important during his diagnosis. He asks questions. Note how much time a physician spends writing out a prescription. And he spends no time at all pointing to diplomas or boasting about cures he's effected. The doctor probes with questions because it is necessary for his diagnosis. Equally as important, he conditions the patient to accept both the diagnosis and the prescription.

Because questions play such an important role in the interview, and because a sale may depend upon how well you ask questions, we will take a close look at this highly learnable skill.

THE VALUE OF QUESTIONING

The single most effective selling tool you have is the ability to ask questions well. People are frequently described as articulate, glib, or having the gift of gab. Others say, "That person ought to be a salesman." But glibness is almost totally irrelevant. What really counts is the ability to ask questions effectively.

By asking questions, you acquire a wealth of useful data. You increase your "intelligence information." You show your interest in the buyer, you draw him or her out, and develop a working relationship. And even more importantly, questions give you three things: control, credibility, and perceived equality.

Control

Consider a classroom setting. In most instances the teacher is in control because the teacher is asking the questions. Now consider again the doctor/patient relationship. The doctor asks the patient 10, 20, or 30 questions. He has complete control of the situation because he's asking the questions. When you ask a question, you are, in effect, saying who's going to talk, and what's going to be talked about. If I ask you, "What do you think of the new Mercedes?" you're not going to talk about the weather. No one else will answer the question. And you're going to speak when I end the question. If you are concerned about prospective buyers talking too much because you have asked them a question, don't worry. Interrupt and ask another question. "You just said something that triggered a thought in my mind (followed by a question)." Maintain control.

Credibility

Questioning also gives you credibility. When a doctor asks incisive, probing, perceptive questions the patient begins to feel that "this guy really knows what he's talking about." As this feeling grows, the patient begins to place himself in the hands of the physician. You can create this same feeling with a potential client.

The most successful sellers do not need to tout themselves. When they ask incisive, perceptive questions, pretty soon the buyer gets the message: "This guy knows what he's doing. He's thorough. He knows the right questions to ask."

Within fifteen minutes you can use questions from and about your field that almost force the client to think you are knowledgeable and competent.

Perceived Equality

Questions also establish a sense of perceived equality. Actually I prefer control because the greater the control the higher the batting average. While a seller may enter a particular selling situation comfortable in his own knowledge and expertise, he may enter another situation with his "hat in his hand," or as an inferior entity. A sense of equality must be established up front.

As a professional in your own field of expertise, you have a vast amount of useful information and data. Further, in most instances you know more about the topic at hand than most people with whom you are speaking. You are due equal standing with the potential buyer. Give the buyer credit for knowing his or her business. But give yourself credit also for knowing yours. Effective questioning will help maintain this attitude during the interview.

LEARNING HOW HE THINKS

Perhaps the most important thing asking questions gives you is a feel for how the buyer thinks. You can discern what his thought processes are, how he gets from point A to point B, and how he *feels* about the topic. If you can understand this, you can deal with him more effectively. This understanding is more important than the hard data the seller will provide to you.

Now lets look at a few fundamental characteristics of the questioning process.

Asking To Ask

By asking the potential client if you may ask questions, you clear the way for an effective interview. In effect, you get permission to probe. Without that permission you may appear to be "pushy," and find yourself being pushed right out the door.

Try something like this. "If I'm going to serve you the way I should, I really need to understand your situation better. I know certain things about your industry, but my experience is that businesses, like people, are all unique. Each situation or business has its own particular facets and I need to understand those which make your's different. Do you mind if I ask you a few questions?"

Approached like that, the prospective client will probably say, "Of course not, go ahead." You will find that people will most often gladly tell you their needs. And all you must do to gain this important knowledge is ask. Specific answers and insight will follow and keep coming as long as you are able to maintain an *empathetic attitude*. Because empathy plays a key role during the interview—your empathy for a potential client and his situation—we will review the concept in detail.

The Art of Asking Questions

Armed with the necessary insight into the theory of questioning, you'll find "open ended" questions an effective and practical approach to the interview process.

Start with general, open-ended questions than encourage discussion, questions that cannot be answered with a "yes," or "no," or with one word. For example, "What did you think of the World Series?" The other person may answer "terrific." To get discussion ask, "What do you think were the two or three really outstanding highlights of the World Series and why?"

One kind of open-ended question used, for example, by IBM salespeople is the *best/worst method*. They ask, "What do you like best about this particular product? Why do you like this, why do you like that? What other things do you like?" Eventually, they'll get around to, "What is it you don't care for?" I once asked the president of a large savings and loan association, "If you could really be objective, if you could stand back and take a look at your firm, what would you say are the primary strengths of this organization?" He immediately said, "People. We have people who are marketing-oriented, people-oriented, customer-oriented, highly competent managers." He went on for two or three minutes. Then I said, "OK, that's one. What's another?" In effect, I was saying, "Go on, there are more, aren't there?" He replied, "Well, I think our facilities are among the finest in the state. If you were to take a poll as to who has the best facilities, I think we'd probably win." After three or four minutes, I asked, "OK, with the same objectivity, what would you say are the areas in which your firm really needs strengthening?"

"Communications," he said. "The people out in the field call the financial people 'bean counters.' Not only that, the bean counters—er, I mean the financial people—call the people out in the field 'peddlers.' I sort of act as an intermediary. They talk through me."

By now I had become the doctor who probes, asking "Does this hurt? How about this?" I was pouring salt on the wound. And the prospect was hurting, telling me exactly what he needed. At the same time, he was telling me what to prescribe.

This is not possible if you spend a lot of time talking about your particular area of expertise *before* you ask probing questions. Hold back on the advantages of your service. First, get the prospect's *needs* and *wants* out on the table.

Focus on the particulars by changing from general, open-ended questions to more specific ones. The purpose of the interview is to move toward that purpose at which you and the prospect *agree on a specific need or want*.

Here are some other types of questions which evoke revealing discussion:

- What is your thinking on. . . ?
- I'd like to better understand your thinking on. . .
- Would you elaborate on that?
- Why are you taking this action?
- What are your greatest areas of potential growth?
- What are the reasons for this?
- Where has your company been? Where is it now? Where is it going?
- If you could step back and be objective, what would you say are your greatest strengths?
- If there was one area that might be strengthened, what would it be and why?
- What would you say are your biggest concerns?
- What do you think needs to be done to improve the situation?
- What are some of the indications that make you feel you could use help?
- What takes up most of your personal attention? Why?
- What are the real reasons you are considering a change? Elaborate.

My experience is the genuine response to this one reveals the most important, emotionally charged beliefs, opinions, positions, and justifications.

One of the greatest strengths the seller can have going for him is the *willingness to walk away from a potential client* if he cannot provide a service that meets the need or want. It is not only an ethical necessity, but a marketing asset that gives credibility and authority to what the seller is saying.

However, the willingness to walk away is quite different from spreading out your services like merchandise in a bazaar and, in effect, saying, "Here's what I've got. See anything you need?" This point is absolutely central to selling. The objective of the interview is *not* to sell. It is to *find out what the prospect needs.* If you arrive at that point, you are likely to make the sale. The good seller first seeks to find problems rather than sell solutions.

Demonstrating Empathy

If questions are the key technique in an interview, the key attitude is empathy. This attitude is crucial in any selling presentation. Demonstrating it should become a habit. Consider the following as our working definition: "The capacity to identify with and understand the other person's point of view."

This does not mean you have to *buy* the other's point of view. It merely means a prospective buyer has his own way of seeing things and his own concept of what is right. He is not only entitled to his point of view, he may elect to use it as a filter to screen anything you say. Whether you agree or not, you must deal with it. That means putting yourself in *his* shoes for a moment, whether or not you like the fit.

A good example of empathy that many professionals understand came from the movie *Patton,* which starred George C. Scott as General George Patton. The Americans and the British had a good deal of difficulty finding Field Marshal Rommel and his army. Finally Patton figures out where Rommel is going to be and posts his men behind trees, crevices, and ridges. Then they wait. And wait. And wait. Finally, sure enough, up rumbles Rommel's army, getting closer and closer with the tanks going along at five or ten miles an hour. Rommel's men are walking behind the tanks in readiness. They get closer and closer and finally Patton orders "Fire!" Then we see exploding tanks, bodies, and a big combat scene with the Americans and Patton gaining the upper hand. Cut to Patton looking through his field glasses. He says, "Rommel, you magnificent bastard, *I read your book*!"

Not literally. Rommel had not written a book describing in detail what he would do in precisely that situation. But Patton had steeped himself in everything Rommel *had* written. Furthermore, he had steeped himself in the material Rommel had read—and would likely influence the German general. Similarly, you must understand a potential buyer from his perspective.

Three Steps to Empathy   First, *perceive each individual's reality, set of values, or viewpoint.* Sometimes it's easy. Sometimes it's not. You and I may have a conversation about politics. I may learn quickly that you lean in a different direction, I may be misled. It's up to me to determine your viewpoint by asking questions. Otherwise, our discussion will be at cross-purposes.

Second, *acknowledge that the prospect is entitled to his viewpoint.* This can be tough. We all make value judgments. We hear somebody talking and think, "That's ridiculous ... ignorant ... stupid ... bigoted." The professional must be able to say, "Not only do I perceive your viewpoint, it's okay for you to have it." All too often we seem to say, "I perceive your viewpoint—*dummy!*"

A universal statement we all hear is, "My business is different." Everybody's is! If we audited five different hospitals over the last year and the sixth says, "Our situation is different," it's easy for us to think, "Baloney, all hospitals are the same." The fact of the matter is, all are different. Each has its own special facets. And, clearly, the seller needs to demonstrate that understanding to the buyer.

To better illustrate the point, consider the graphic shown on page 70. While one person may see a bird bath in this picture, another may see two people facing one another. That doesn't make one right and the other wrong! The first actually *sees* a bird bath. It's as real to him as the two faces are to the other person. This picture is "really" whatever you see—a Texas Longhorn, an upsidedown vacuum cleaner attachment, or a martini glass. Your business is also however you see it.

You may have more information and more experience than the client. You may want to change his point of view. But to deny his viewpoint, or his right to it, is not the way to approach professional services. Keep your judgments and evaluations to yourself. First, ferret out and fully understand the prospective buyer's point of view. For you, as a professional, to grant the client a right to his own opinion does not mean sacrificing your ethics or lowering your

standards. It means only that you understand. Certain things are very real to the client. Whether or not these things conform with objective reality is not important at this point.

However, the professional must avoid making any commitment to the "reality" of the client's viewpoint. Your attitude should not be, "I see what you mean and you are absolutely right!" It should be, "Tell me about it. I'm easy to talk to." Only when you've taken these first two steps—recognizing the prospect's viewpoint and acknowledging that he has a right to it—can you move on to the third step.

Third, *get inside the prospect's head*. See matters from his viewpoint, with his background and conditioning. This does not mean agreement. Nor does it mean *sympathy*. Feeling sorry for the client blurs your vision. It gets in the way of good decisions. Say, in effect, "I understand your anger. I don't blame you for getting mad." Don't say, "I feel just as angry as you." *Sympathy is not service*. And it isn't a good marketing or selling tactic. The buyer doesn't want you to feel sorry for him. He wants to be understood.

Empathy helps you discover the causes of the trouble with the searchlight of insight. Through empathy, one person comes to appreciate another person's feelings without becoming so emotionally involved that his judgment is affected. The Sioux Indians expressed empathy when they prayed, "Great Spirit, help us never to judge another until we have walked for two weeks in his moccasins."* Finally, empathy is the key to leadership. It unlocks the dreams in the hearts of others so the leader can help make those dreams come true.

We have spent a considerable amount of time thus far on asking questions, soliciting information, and practicing empathy. The chapter would be incomplete without consideration of receiving, and more importantly, grasping the information. That is, to listening and *actually hearing* what's being said.

Listening and Hearing

It's not enough to just ask the right questions. You must *listen* and *hear*. There's a distinction between the two. Listening is the receipt of information. Hearing is understanding. Hearing is deeper. It's grasping the innuendo, subtleties, and emotions.

Practice considering the other person as an individual, and *listen* to him. This means *really* listening. At the next party you attend, look around. Everyone is either talking or awaiting a chance to talk. *No one is listening*. There are certain techniques that will enable you to hear better.

First, I recommend physical and mental stillness. If I turn pages, move, or think about other things while you're speaking to me, I cannot grasp what you are saying. I need to read your eyes and your facial expressions. The best way I can do that is to still my mind and body. When the prospect talks, still yourself—physically and mentally.

Second, make a slight movement—an inch or six inches— toward the buyer. This leaning forward with elbows on knees, saying, "Well, that's really interesting. Tell me more about that." As you move closer, you become more intent on what the buyer has to say, and the buyer begins to perceive your greater interest.

Third is eye contact—not for minutes at a time but for several

*From *The New Book of the Art of Living* by Wilferd A. Peterson, published by Simon and Schuster.

seconds. This should be done frequently. Several years ago the University of Chicago conducted a series of programs that concluded the eyes really are "the windows of the soul." We blink more when lying and less when telling the truth. The pupils expand when we tell the truth and contract when we lie. So it's very much to the seller's advantage to frequently look directly into the buyer's eyes. You may see more, and you will also seem more trustworthy to the buyer. But it's a two-edged sword. You are making yourself vulnerable to having your "soul" looked into.

Another help is nodding. A nod says, "Tell me more, go on, continue, I am receiving your messages." You're not necessarily saying, "I agree or disagree." But you're helping to maintain the conversation. Remember, the more the client talks—about almost anything, although preferably the special business at hand—the more you learn.

Fourth, hold back your evaluations. Ultimately you are paid to make evaluations and decisions, but not while ferreting out needs and wants. Use, "I see" or, "Really?" or, "Tell me about that," or "You certainly feel strongly about that," rather than telling him or her they're right or wrong. Ask many open-ended questions that force the buyer to open up and reveal his hand. Make yourself easy to talk to. The more the prospective buyer talks, the smarter you get and the closer you get.

I'll remember for a long time a conversation I had with my then 16-year-old son. It was 11:20 when he popped into the house one February morning. I was working in my office and wondered what in the world he was doing home from school at this time of day. He said, "Mom wanted the car—now she doesn't."

I asked, "What classes do you have left today?"
He said, "Spanish and some kind of shop."
"What are you getting in Spanish?"
"I think I'm getting an A," he said.
"How would you like to go skiing—right now?"
"Sure!"

Ten minutes later we were on the road. He had spent all of his schooling in parochial school and had just switched over to the public high school, despite our reservations. As we pulled out onto the freeway, I said "Now that you've seen both systems of schooling, how do you see the differences?"

My son said there was more discipline at the parochial school. But sometimes the discipline was stupid—discipline for the sake of discipline, he said. On the other hand, the public school could use a little more of it.

I asked, "What about the kids, the caliber of kids you are dealing with?"

He responded by saying this and that. He mentioned dope. I asked if there was more or less. He said it differed.

"Like what are the differences?" I asked.

We went on and on for one and a half hours. I never said, "Son, we don't accept that in our family," or, that something was good or bad. All I did was ask open-ended questions and gave no evaluations . . . other than to show interest in his thoughts and feelings. Two things happened. Dad got smarter because he was being educated about what's "so" with his son. Also, we got closer.

Every time you get prospective buyers of your services to open up and say how they really feel two things happen. You get smarter, and you get closer.

In order to demonstrate certain interviewing techniques and even specific questions, I created an interview between two people, Mike and Jerry. Jerry is a marketing director for a medical products company. He knows Mike as having a reputation of putting on quality sales training and personal development seminars. The two have only talked on the phone prior to their meeting. Mike's public image with Jerry has already been established by third party support. They meet at Jerry's place of business. Mike's opening has taken place and he moves Jerry into the interview phase of a track to run on.

Mike: If I'm going to serve you the way you ought to be served, I need to understand a little bit about who will be there, the thrust of the meeting, the theme, and some things about your company. So, would you mind if if I ask you a few questions about your firm. Let me start with the firm itself.

Jerry: Go ahead.

Mike: I know a few things about your company. I know you make medical products.

Jerry: We probably have about 60 percent of the market of plastic disposable medical products.

Mike: But I need to know a little bit more about what you do. Can you tell me?

Jerry: Well, I guess I could say—you mentioned theme. We do have a theme for this program and it's . . .

Mike: Do you mind if I take a few notes?

Jerry: Oh, no. Go ahead. The theme for this program is Challenge for the 80s. We have been very successful in the marketplace, and we recognize that a lot of competition is coming on stream and its going to make it more and more tough for our guys to do their jobs. We thought we'd bring them all together. This is the first time, by the way, we've ever done this. We thought we'd bring all our salesmen in to the home office. They are scattered all over the country.

Mike: Excuse me. You mentioned salesmen. Are they all men?

Jerry: Yes.

Mike: Will they be bringing spouses?

Jerry: Yes. Part of the intent here is to say to them, "We recognize that you're out there. You are only communicated to by letter and phone, and we want you to know what the home office looks like. We'd like you to meet some of the people in personnel and finance that you are dealing with. So what we'd really like to do is bring you out here, give you a week of fun in the California sun." Let them hear a presentation from some of our technical people.

Mike: So there will be several programs they will be going through over the period of the week. Some technical. And will there also be several outside resources?

Jerry: No, no. We're just planning to have one outside resource on the program. It's partly social, it's partly instructional and about twenty salespeople and their wives will be present.

Mike: You've really made a financial commitment haven't you?

Jerry: Yes, yes.

Mike: Can you describe for me in general terms the line of products these people deal with? Does each person have all products for example?

Jerry: No. The sales staff is divided into three areas: (1) plastic disposable medical products, (2) cardiopulmonary products, and (3) implantable devices.

Mike: I'm not sure of this, did you say that the salesmen themselves are divided into three groups handling those three different products.

Jerry: Yes—three groups, three different product areas.

Mike: And there are only twenty of them! Around the world?

Jerry: No, in the U.S. This is domestic sales. We have distributors internationally.

Mike: Okay, it still seems like a few number of people handling an enormous volume.

Jerry: Yes, I would say that's true.

Mike: May I ask how these people are paid?

Jerry: Both salary and commission. A very competitive salary base and an extremely competitive commission base.

Mike: Would it be fair to ask for a range—what kind of income do these people make?

Jerry: I think a two- to three-year sales representative, who has been with this company and is acquainted with his territory could expect $40-45,000.

Mike: Now, let's use the number 40. Of the 40, what would be the upside range? Do some people make 80—100?

Jerry: I would say 50-55.

Mike: Using the number 50, how much of that would be salary and how much of that would be commission?

Jerry: 60 percent salary, 30 percent commission.

Mike: There is a reason I asked that question. I'm convinced that if the commission part is not more than 20-25 percent, by that I mean 30, 35, 50 and even 100 percent, if it's not that much and more than it isn't a very good commission arrangement, and there isn't enough motivation. So, I'm pleased to see that. What would be the age range of these people?

Jerry: The youngest man that we have is 24 years old and the oldest is 53 with a median of about 30.

Mike: So it's on the younger side, isn't it?

Jerry: Yes, it is.

Mike: Typically, how many years of experience do they have with the firm?

Jerry: I would say about four. We are a pretty young firm.

Mike: That's one of the things that is coming out in this. I guess I knew it but it doesn't ring a bell until you ask the kinds of questions that clarify it. From your earlier comments, do I understand the purpose of this meeting is a form of preventive medicine to gear up for what you think is coming.

Jerry: Yes, I think preventive medicine is a good way to think of it. When we first conceived of the annual meeting we used words like, "build a team," "to build a feeling that we are all in this together," "to break bread with one another," share, camaraderie."

Mike: Closeness?

Jerry: Yes, and I think I would emphasize more than anything letting the salesmen know this home office cares about them. By the way, you know, our guys are required to be away from their families probably 60 percent of the time.

Mike: That much, huh?

Jerry: In the last year that's the way it has been.

Mike: What would be a typical week?

Jerry: A typical week would be three days on the road.

Mike: So he might go out Monday night and be back Tuesday, Wednesday, Thursday.

Jerry: Come back Wednesday night maybe, or Thursday night.

Mike: Well, yes, if there are only twenty people doing this kind of volume, and let's assume that the volume number was 20 million. With twenty people doing the 20 million, they would be on the road a lot.

Jerry: So that entered into our thinking as we were planning the meeting. That's why the wives are coming.

Mike: Excuse the interruption, but one of the things that, again, becomes clarified is I think that is a particularly good move to bring the wives because the company in certain instances is seen as competition to the wives. And this will allay that. This will help soothe that a little bit and show that it is the three of them, the man, the wife and the company. I congratulate you on that because I think it's an important part of it.

Jerry: I think you hit it right on the head. That's what we're looking for. In fact, we've planned putting a red rose on the pillows in the hotel room when the wives come.

Mike: Tell me more about what is being specifically done for the women.

Jerry: A fashion show will be an event just for them. They are going to be included—it's not specifically for them—but they are going to be included in some of the presentations that are made. The women are going to be asked to stand at the gala dinner we're planning and the president of the firm will offer a toast to the wives themselves. So they are going to feel very much a part of it. And when you said the company is often deemed a competitor by the wives, I think that because this is so, we really want to address that part of it. So when we talked with you about the presentation you might make to us we'd like to think that the women will be present.

Mike: What do you think is the temperature of the salesmen in regards to coming to this week-long meeting?

Jerry: I think it was probably a good mix of reactions. We have some new people aboard who are probably very excited about coming. Some of the older people, with five or six years, who have been here on the West Coast training or what have you—by the way, we're showing off our new building. I don't know if you know it or not, but we're moving into our new headquarters probably a week before we have this meeting. I guess I feel there will be mixed reactions. We're not telling them a lot by the way. We're trying to entice them a little bit. We've asked them to send pictures of the children, for instance. We want to include in a program, a booklet we are having made, pictures of the salesmen's children. And they don't know why we're asking for pictures of their children.

Mike: Yes, yes.

Jerry: The regional managers, there are two of them, are hearing from the sales representatives. They are being asked a lot of questions: "Well, what's going on?", "What are we doing?" So we are playing it kind of cute. Does that answer your question?

Mike: Yes. I think I have seen every kind of reaction from all company meetings. Anywhere from, "Oh, my God, another one of these," to curiosity, to "this is interfering with my production time." You name it. I think I hear you saying all of those are being represented.

Jerry: I think when they step off the plane that will be in the air.

Mike: Yes. What is it you have in mind for the kind of thing that I do?

Jerry: Well, we began asking some of the people we knew who had held meetings like this in the past. We first asked Fred Wilson to tell us what experience he has had with outside resources. We asked him to give us names of anyone he'd think would be good to present to both men and women. Your name was one of the three names he gave us.

Mike: One of the things you've stressed several times is that the meeting I would be conducting would be a husband and wife meeting, rather than just the salesmen. I'm glad for that. I'm also interested in what Fred had to tell you about myself and what it is I do.

Jerry: He said that he had personally seen you make a presentation before a company in which the spouses were involved and that you seem to, and I remember his comments specifically, that you seemed to have the women more involved than even the men during the meeting. He just liked what he saw going on. He gave you a very strong endorsement.

Mike: Do you know what the topic of that particular meeting was?

Jerry: Communications.

Mike: Yes, that doesn't surprise me, because I do a session on communication that is very, well, I like to think it is enlightening. I like to think it is entertaining, and it is certainly audience-involving. What I typically do is make a point, support it with an example, and get involvement. Sometimes I invite people up to the front of the room and have them do things, and sometimes I don't. It kind of depends on what we develop here together. So can I assume communication would be one of the topics that may be something that you are looking for?

Jerry: Well, I think that's a great possibility.

Mike: Let me toss another idea at you. My viewpoint is that management's biggest challenge is what I call "alignment." When I use the term alignment I mean when you *get* the people involved. By aligning the personal goals of your salesmen with those of this headquarters, you get a sense of alignment. It is things like "pulling together." It is things like teamwork. It is synergism. As I say, that is any management group's biggest challenge. Because when you get it, I think the rest of the ballgame is over. Everybody is seeing how you can get what you want by aligning himself with the unit. Well, I do a session on that and I'm wondering if that seems to fit the theme?

Jerry: Yes, we certainly have a well-understood system throughout the company. Our people are oriented to setting goals, and to my knowledge I haven't thought of ever suggesting this term alignment that you used in relation to goal-setting with the company. Are you saying, as it applies to the individual?

Mike: As it applies to the entire unit. If you can get the individual aligning his goals with the unit, I'm saying it makes MBO (management by objectives) programs work. One of the things I sense in other companies, and I don't know if it's the case here, is that salesmen feel isolated. They feel like they are out in the field, they are a voice alone in the wilderness.

Jerry: Exactly.

Mike: And I feel, one of the things that is frequently expressed, or I have uncovered as a result of a lot of interviewing, is that if you can make those people out there feel closer to the team, a part of it, you have a better man and that's where this sense of alignment frequently fits. And I'm wondering if it doesn't just fit into this theme well.

Jerry: Do you see the wives fitting in?

Mike: Well, again, I see that the wives have a different kind of isolation. And that is that the company is not only out there someplace on the West Coast but it's the thing that keeps my husband from me. So, yes, to the degree that husband and wife and firm all see themselves as aligned, what I call this thing called synergism. By the way, there's a great analogy I like to use. Imagine I have two bars of metal in my hand, one of which is a magnet and one of which is merely a bar of metal. And the bar of metal and the magnet are composed of the same chemcial ingredients, with one difference. In the bar of metal the molecules are nonaligned. In the magnet, the moleclues are aligned, in a to-and-fro fashion. And as a result you have an additional force and an additional power that is missing in the other bar. When you get that within a company, and that is the husbands, wives, and the firm aligned, you get synergism. Where one and one no longer equals two, it equals 3, 4, or more.

Jerry: That's interesting.

Mike: There is a way I believe of introducing that and implementing it into a program that almost creates a greater responsibility or obligation toward the three units. I'd like to propose that that be carefully considered for this program.

Jerry: I like everything you've said about this alignment presentation. If you could do that I'd prefer that to the communication idea we discussed earlier.

Mike: We have not discussed the amount of time that is being allotted for this.

Jerry: We're looking for—are you talking about the presentation for wives and husbands?

Mike: Yes.

Jerry: No more than two hours. I guess I should ask you if you do your program in two hours.

Mike: Well, that's an obvious question that should be asked here. Is this going to be, have you considered whether it's going to be used as a kick off or as an ending?

Jerry: So far, in the tentative itinerary, it looks about midway through the program. There has been some social things, some working activities. The women have attended a fashion show, they've had a luncheon. The men have been meeting with engineers and administrative people.

Mike: To what degree have they been told outright now that they want the salesmen and their wives to be felt more a part of the . . .

Jerry: They have not been.

Mike: Okay. You know what might be a consideration? You might have that very message given to them by the president of the firm as an opener. Like when they get there Sunday night, or Monday morning, or whenever they get there. Make it a formal thing: . . . You are an important part of our family. You are our extremities, you are our limbs, both of you Mr. and Mrs. Brown, and we want you to know that this company depends greatly on you, and thinks highly of what you do and the contribution you are making. I think that message needs to be pounded home hard.

Jerry: We are going to have a cocktail reception party planned for the day of arrival. The president and the staff will be there mingling . . .

Mike: Is there going to be a formal presentation or is that going to be the next morning?

Jerry: The next morning. Correct.

Mike: At one of those two things I would strongly suggest that the president of the firm give that kind of message in a five-minute way. I think I could embellish on that, either right after that or some time during the week. In a two-hour session I could do an hour and a half on communications and about half an hour on the alignment concept. And really try to cement that, try to make those people even more closely allied to the firm and a part of it.

Jerry: I think that's a good consideration.

Mike: There is another consideration. I'm kind of glad that you picked communications because once again, almost without exception, every sales group that I have ever had the opportunity to deal with in terms of how it relates to the company feels communications are not good. So I'm kind of asking on a scale of one to ten how does that seem to fit in this instance.

Jerry: Could be better. Could be better.

Mike: Now with you representing the headquarters and they feel the communications is not what it should be from field to in-house . . .

Jerry: I would give anything to have a few expense reports in on time.

Mike: I am willing to bet there are several salesmen in the field who feel that the problem is not from them to you or to the headquarters, but from the headquarters to them. Have you done any work in the area of communications, any training?

Jerry: Oh, no. We have not.

Mike: That's interesting.

Jerry: We've been so busy just moving products.

Mike: Just keeping up with orders. Terrible problem you have!

Jerry: That's right. So now we did want to pause and say, "Let's get everybody together, shake some hands, solidify that force, that salesforce and the Challenge 82." And stay at the pace we are. Things are starting to bottle up. We are starting to face some backorders on a slide scale and we want to make sure we are heading in the right direction. Pull together and take this time out. We think it's necessary to take this time out.

Mike: You say you have done no training between headquarters and the field force?

Jerry: No. We do a lot of technical training on the introduction of products and we have just a pretty quick—what we do is once the man is acquainted with the product, there's a period of teaming up with an experienced salesman who makes calls with him. And that's the extent of our training. As far as the topic communication—no, we have done nothing.

Mike: Yet, these people are fairly young, so even the experienced people may not have been exposed to a lot in the areas of communication.

Jerry: Unless they picked up a course with another company.

Mike: Have you found that area to be much of a stumbling block? Have you run into any specific problem from headquarters out? Am I asking the right person for that?

Jerry: Uh, what do you mean?

Mike: Well, I'm thinking the sales managers are the people that would have a firsthand answer to that question. The people in-house who interface, at least by phone, to the sales force on a regular basis, I wonder how they would answer the question about the communications from field to headquarters.

Jerry: I think that you could talk—about everybody that you would talk to would give you the same answer, that it could be improved upon. But I don't know that anybody's talking about it as a great problem of any kind. I think the alienation that one might feel out in Omaha or wherever is stronger than any feelings about poor communications. I might complain about a sales report now and then and jump up and down, but that's not foremost on my mind. We'll get them in ultimately. What I'm looking for is that feeling of being a part of something which is more than a leased car, an expense account, waiting in lines in airports, and delays. So while the communications topic is kind of generically good, your comments about your alignment of the organization with the person struck me as being closer to the mark I guess.

Mike: Now, my question is should I weight that differently? I was talking about an hour and a half on communications and a half hour on alignment. The alignment thing is in itself an hour or an hour and fifteen minutes. Let's say an hour. Should I weight it 50/50? Would that be more appropriate?

Jerry: Possibly even more than that. Maybe 60/40 with alignment. I'm not familiar with how you would approach that but if you could I would say that I would personally favor your thinking alignment as carrying more weight in your presentation.

Mike: Should it be 100 percent?

Jerry: I think that would be a good consideration. I think so. We may not want to determine that now, but I'm not opposed to the idea.

Mike: From this, I hear you saying is what has greater fit is this pulling together, the teamwork, the alignment, feeling a part of, in lieu of the communications.

Jerry: Yes. That's the idea. I'd like that.

At this time, Mike has effectively accomplished the goal of the interview: a specific need/want has surfaced. Mike would then move more actively into his responding presentation and satisfy these needs/wants.

SUMMARY

The purpose of the interview is to get the buyer's specific needs or wants out on the table and elaborated. This is essential. It may take five minutes, five hours, or maybe five meetings. But do not proceed further until you are sure of what he needs. Project an attitude that suggests, "This is your turn to talk. I'm going to do my best to make it easy for you to tell me what's important to you, Mr. Buyer." Be empathic.

Use open-ended questions to focus on the most urgent need—the place where it hurts.

Listen, but above all, *hear* during the interview.

The interview is the buyer's time, his turn to talk, to reveal, to hurt, and to educate you. Make it easy for him or her to do so by asking questions well and listening empathically. Now you're ready for your turn—*the Responding Presentation.*

7

The
Responding
Presentation

The responding presentation is aptly named. It is your response to what has surfaced during the interview phase of the selling presentation. It is more than a mere "presentation." It is, in the medical analogy, the time for you to be the expert and prescribe the best course of action, the solution, or the cure.

The degree to which you have been able to pinpoint specific needs and wants during the interview equates to how specific you can be in your response. A well-conducted interview, which surfaces specific needs and wants, allows you to be the specialist as you respond rather than a generalist. Buyers like specialists! It is the difference between firing a sawed-off shotgun at a target and hoping you hit the bull's-eye, as opposed to taking careful, marksman-like aim with a target rifle. The responding presentation is your chance to say, "Here's what we ought to do. Here's how we ought to do it. And here's when we ought to do it." In addition, you'll be able to support your recommendations with targeted benefits and credible reasons for doing whatever action or commitment you suggest.

WHY PEOPLE BUY

People buy based on emotions. And they support their "buying" with logic. This is not only true for cars, houses, clothes, appliances, and so on, it is true for professional services and ideas. The two biggest investments most people make—cars and houses—are almost always purchased based on emotion, and rationalized with logic afterwards. Understanding and working with this natural circumstance is an important selling technique.

When selling to people's emotions, the seller has to be "bought" by the buyer most of the time. Sellers must sell themselves to other people before they get an opportunity to begin selling what it is they're offering. This idea is difficult for many people to grasp. For instance, consider this professional tax accountant:

"I spent twenty years studying taxation and tax legislation. I work on some of the most complex tax cases in the world. I am selling service and expertise!" Wrong! Before he can sell that service and expertise, he must first sell himself. Sell yourself first, and what you're offering second. Everything else you have to offer will be easier to sell if the buyer "buys" you. Unfortunately, the reverse is also true! People emotionally "buy" other people, their ideas and services, based on likeability, credibility, trust, friendliness, rapport, and "chemistry." Only after these intangibles are present can you reasonably expect to bring about a favorable action or commitment.

The responding presentation consists of your providing the answers in whatever form they take—a verbal recommendation, a nicely prepared written proposal, or supporting evidence. And as you provide the data, you and the buyer move quite naturally toward an agreement or concurrence. Although we treat the natural conclusion as a separate part of the track to run on in the following chapter, the ideal situation is to have the responding presentation and natural conclusion blend into one another without any drama. Buying should not be a terribly dramatic decision for the buyer. It should be a natural result of what you and the buyer have agreed on.

During the previous chapter on interviewing, we stressed the importance of your role as a listener. In the responding presentation stage, your role is that of presenter. One thing you probably will not want to present is written proposals and documents. There are reasons why you should not.

WRITTEN PROPOSALS AND SUPPORTIVE DOCUMENTS

A written proposal serves one purpose. It contains evidence to support your claims. Any less than that is insufficient, and more is padding. The same is true for brochures and other forms of advertising you may be inclined to use in a responding presentation. The use of printed documents in the sales presentation is a touchy business. More often than not, the use of such materials is troublesome—they can get in your way. One primary consideration to keep in mind is that brochures, pamphlets, fancy proposals and audio-visual shows, don't sell—people do. These items should be considered for what they are, tools, vehicles, or media that supports you and what you have to say. They are good confirming documents. They make nice "leave-behinds."

One of the major drawbacks of placing too much time, money, and effort on written materials is that people don't read them. Millions of hours and dollars are spent on written proposals on which buying decisions are not primarily based. People buy you first, and then what you're selling. The key to whether or not they "buy" you, is how you conduct your oral presentation. And more importantly, before you *respond* with an oral presentation, they look at how effectively you have been able to conduct the all-important *interview*. The two are closely interrelated.

Although I downplay the role of written documents, I feel they are necessary. The absence of them, especially when everybody else uses them, would be too detrimental to you and your business. They help give you visibility and exposure, but their purpose is not to sell in your place. Written proposals, brochures, and other documents should not be relied upon to carry the burden in a selling presentation. That is one task that is best left to the individual.

Think how often the selling presentation has been depicted as a salesmen entering a room with his bag of tricks—flip chart, slide projector, chalkboard, product samples—and how at the designated moment he opens his mouth and "delivers his spiel." At another designated moment during his presentation he passes out bulky proposals to the participants in the meeting. He reviews some of the key points, and then concludes by saying, "Are there any questions?"

Generally, there aren't any. They all shake hands, and someone says, "We'll look this stuff over and give you a call later in the month." End of presentation.

That's not the kind of presentation we're talking about here. Rather than emphasizing bells and whistles our emphasis is on the person to person, eyeball-to-eyeball meeting where printed matter and actual product samples are kept to a minimum.

When you hand people printed items or other things in meetings, their attention shifts away from you to what you have placed in their hands. You're out of it and you've just lost control. In a responding presentation you don't want to be out of it: You want to *be* it! Hold these things back, and if you think it is absolutely necessary to give out something during your selling presentation—or if you are asked to—place a copy of whatever it is in their hands and try at least to sit alongside them as you guide them through the piece. Walk them through it.

If you find you are losing their attention to printed matter and they are no longer hearing you, be still. Silence your body and your tongue and hold back until you once again have their attention. Sometimes, our own enthusiasm and mental inertia makes this the hardest thing in the world to do. The ideal situation is to respond verbally with a bare minimum of written documents. Then, only after you've arrived at some concurrence or agreement, should you use material as a "leave-behind." It is my view that in a responding presentation, it is better to be empty-handed than to go in with an arsenal of four-color gobbledegook and gibberish.

EVIDENCE

During a responding presentation, you may want to provide additional evidence in the form of testimonials, samples, trial results, and so on, especially if the person to whom you are selling knows the person who gave you the testimonial. You might mention that person's name and what he had to say about you or your service, or you might leave behind a copy of a reference letter or note you were given.

Another option is to mail the person testimonials after you've had a meeting that did not bring about a favorable action or commitment. Along these lines, I think it is also valuable to mail articles you think they might be interested in, possibly a book, or any number of things that make you appear thoughtful, on the ball, and really interested. The purpose of all this, of course, is to stay close in the hopes of getting another chance at bat when the time comes.

But keep in mind, the world's greatest endorsement doesn't make your sale automatic. In fact, take the position that "no sale is automatic." Don't allow printed documents to take the place of the *you* in the responding presentation—ever.

The most direct way to determine whether or not the buyer is with you during or toward the end of the responding presentation is to ask questions like, "Is this hitting the nail on the head?" or, "Is this making sense to you?" Then quiet yourself. Be still. And wait for the answer. Your opening got the other person's attention. Your thorough and effective interview surfaced not only general needs and wants, but very specific ones. You have now orally responded with a specific solution that matches the buyer's need, and now it's time to ask, "Does this solution make sense?"

If they say, "It makes a lot of sense," you can move on to a natural conclusion. If they say, "No," Stop. Red flag. Alert. You want to be right on, not just close. You may even ask to have the buyer help you adjust your presentation to even better meet his needs. You are then back into the interview stage. Once again, you play the role of the probing, inquiring, helpful doctor. Using open-ended questions and getting the buyer to open up, will help surface the real objections or reasons for hesitating.

Once you get objections—the real ones—out on the table, you can at least deal with them. Many people wrongly stay in a responding mode, almost debating the buyer on the objection points, one for one. To see who's "right" you should be reinterviewing the buyer.

About Objections

Here are three thoughts about objections:

1. Regain the buyer's attention.
2. Help him specify the nature of the objection through questioning.
3. As needs surface, fill them.

The philosophical attitude you want to create and maintain throughout the responding presentation, especially when you are talking about objections, is that it is me and you, Mr. Buyer, against the problem. It is not me against you.

There are other important attitudes about objections that I think are worth noting:

1. There are bound to be some of them. They come with the territory.
2. See them as opportunities.
3. Don't argue about them.
4. An objection met is another tumbler in the lock. Meeting them leads you closer to the sale.

Chances are, you've heard most of the objections about you and/ or what you're selling before anyway. Be prepared. Here is an opportunity—without cramming anything down anybody's throat— to offer proof and supporting statements, testimonials, or provide statistics.

The key thing to remember is that when an objection surfaces, do not proceed with your responding presentation. Adapt to the situation, interview the subject of the resistance, and only when you have reached some satisfactory degree of concurrence or agreement, proceed to the natural conclusion.

RULES OF THE GAME

Remember this maxim about buyers. Buyers tell the truth. They tell half truths. They tell what they think is the truth, but isn't. And they tell lies.

The best position to find yourself in during any selling presentation is to find yourself dealing with the truth. But it isn't always easy to distinguish between what is and what isn't the truth. Consider some rules of the selling game that buyers think of as the truth.

1. We'll decide based on the written proposal.
2. No calls between 11 a.m. and 2 p.m. Monday-Thursday.
3. All bids will be kept in confidence.
4. We treat all vendors (sellers) the same.

Hogwash! Rules—in selling and in most things—are negotiable. You'll find as you get close with people, the hard and fast rules they once shoved at you are no longer important to them.

> Let's get together to understand the proposal guidelines.
>
> Sure, call me during lunch.
>
> Say, this XYZ bid is a little lower than yours, but if you can shave a few bucks off, it's yours.

And by the way, winners are always treated better than others, usually before they win. People like to deal with winners. As is usually the case, most rules are not truthfully rules at all, but merely "guidelines."

During your responding presentation, if you play by the rules, you'll lose. I'm not saying break them. I'm saying if you can find ways around the rules, do it. Besides, buyers break their own rules. Rules are negotiable. So negotiate them!

During your responding presentation, you want the buyer to be as truthful with you as he wants you to be with him. It is necessary to know, now that you've committed yourself to "presenting," whether or not the buyer is with you and with the course of action you're recommending. You need to know—honestly and directly— if you are approaching an agreement or concurrences.

SUMMARY

The responding presentation consists of your providing answers in whatever form they take—a verbal recommendation, written proposal, evidence, contract, and so on—which addresses the needs or wants that surfaced in the interviewing process. While your role during the interview is *question-asker,* your role in the responding presentation is *presenter*—the one with the *answers*.

Remember, *people* sell. Brochures, pamphlets, proposals, etc., only reinforce at best.

Use evidence wisely, and when discussing "rules" with buyers, remember, rules are almost always negotiable! One way to determine if your responding presentation is on track, is to ask the buyer directly, "Is this making sense to you?" Then quiet yourself. Be still. Read them. And be willing to drop back into the interview phase if you feel it is necessary or the prudent thing to do. A good responding presentation should lead comfortably—even naturally—to a mutually satisfactory agreement or conclusion.

The Natural
Conclusion

The natural conclusion should be made a part of, not apart from, the responding presentation. The purpose of the natural conclusion is to gain a favorable action or commitment from the buyer. What you want is something that is agreeable to both of you. If this doesn't happen, the next best thing is to keep the door open, to schedule another meeting, so that you can at least stay in the batter's box.

There should be nothing dramatic about the natural conclusion, or close. It should be as its name implies, *natural*. Closes are not climaxes, nor should they be. As a part of a total sequence of events, closes should be the mutually satisfactory result or outcome of the whole selling presentation.

The Natural Conclusion consists of these four parts.

1. A brief summary of specific needs and wants.
2. A brief summary of the solutions/answers to those needs and wants.
3. The closing question or statement that evokes the favorable action or commitment.
4. Handling any objections that may come up.

AN ASSUMPTIVE ATTITUDE

With natural conclusions, I think an attitude of assumptiveness is most important. Let's review the track to run on. Your opening accomplished its objective; it established value in you, the topic, or the moment. The buyer paid close attention to you and what you had to say. Your interview succeeded to bring very specific needs and wants out on the table. You asked the right questions, maintained equality and credibility, and listened attentively to the answers. You really understood the problem/opportunity. And you were perceived as such. Your responding presentation was right on target, specifically addressing the buyers wants and needs.

Having done all this well, you should have an attitude of assumptiveness about reaching a natural conclusion. In fact, the attitude to take is that it would be unnatural if you didn't reach a mutually satisfying conclusion!

The doctor/patient analogy is a good one. When the doctor comes to a conclusion (answers/solutions) about a patient's condition, and responds (prescribes a course of action), he certainly assumes the patient will accept (favorable commitment or action) his recommendation. The same is true for you, your ideas, and services. Without conveying an, "I know I've got it sewed up," or "It's in the bag" kind of attitude, you have to transmit a feeling of confidence, a naturalness, an "assumptiveness" about reaching the natural conclusion. Most sales opportunities that are not cashed in happen either because the person is timid about asking, so he asks ineffectively, or because he doesn't ask at all! It's like hitting a home run, rounding the bases and then running into the dugout from third, without touching the plate. Sure you hit the home run, but untill you touch home base you haven't scored. A doctor never says, "Do you think you'd like to take this medication?" If he did, you'd get another doctor. You want, and expect, your doctor to say, "Here's what you ought to do," period. An attitude of assumptiveness is most important for a natural conclusion.

TIME IS OF THE ESSENCE

The best time for a doctor to get a patient to commit, or a lawyer to get a client to commit, is when the patient or client has already invested himself in terms of time, effort, emotional energy, and money, and is in the doctor's or lawyer's office hurting and needing help. If you don't get to them then, anything can happen. At the very least you've lost "buying momentum," which is invaluable, and at the worst, you could be dropped out of the race. Closing is easy if you do a whole lot of things before hand. Scoring is easy when you touch all the bases.

The longer the time period between the responding presentation and the recommended action or favorable commitment, the greater the likelihood for a blown deal. Another vital factor is to allow as little time as possible to elapse between a "yes" and the start of work. Too many things can happen in a month or two. Do something now! Get engaged, get the buyer involved and obligated following a yes decision. To make sure you don't blow any deals in the close, follow these three steps.

1. *Summarize Needs and Wants*   Don't let the opportunity to close get away when you are confident you've covered all the bases. Move in. The first thing you want to do is summarize the needs and wants—the hurts, problems, concerns, and situations—which surfaced during the interview. The process should not take longer than a minute or two. It is a clear statement or statements of facts or strongly held beliefs. The summary is confirmation.

2. *Summarize Solutions/Answers*   During the responding presentation you reached concurrence and agreement on specific solutions and answers. Again, to confirm, strengthen, and reinforce the answers, summarize them with an air of assumptiveness.

3. *Ask A Closing Question Or Make A Closing Statement*   At this point, ask a closing question that will elicit a "yes" response, or offer a statement that confirms your recommended course of action, solution, or commitment. Your question should not be open-ended but something specific and direct. And after you ask the question—"We're in agreement that we're going to do such and such?"—be still, wait for the answer.

The calender is an excellent closing tool. It works for any number of people in a wide variety of occupations and professions. Nowadays, practically everyone keeps some kind of appointment or planning calendar. Use yours to close sales, to reach natural conclusions. Ask the buyer to look at his or her calendar as you do the same and see how your schedules match to do the agreed upon work or perform whatever service or function you have sold him/her. Focusing on the time element takes attention off the decision-making process, which can also help you.

Alternative Closes

Another tool that works effectively when closing is an offering of alternative choices. Which of the two solutions fits the buyer's operation best? "We can start day after tomorrow or at the end of the month—which works best for you?"

Buyers like options. Buyers like choices. And most of all, they like to feel they've *bought* rather than *been sold*.

Following the steps outlined in a track to run on makes closing easy. Closing is as it is supposed to be: a mutual and natural conclusion; a harmonious agreement that two people are comfortable with. Most people prefer the word, "agreement" to "contract," but it depends on what it is you're selling. Be sensitive to "language" not only during the conclusion but during the entire selling process.

WHEN THEY STILL SAY "NO"

Sometimes, when even after your best effort, the buyer still says, "no," there are two things you can do.

1. Ask them to specify their reasons. In effect, drop back into an interview. Get them to surface their needs again and respond— meet their objections as an ally, as one trying to help.

2. Propose (or create) a "next step" with the buyer to stay "close."

3. If you fail to win the commitment or favorable action—let it go cordially and tastefully. The secret to letting go is to let go of that particular moment. But at the same time, create reasons to stay close. Try to get another opportunity to get to bat at another time. Personal, nonsales-related visits, a note or letter, a copy of an article that you know they'd like, or a book will keep you close. And be patient. More often than not, another chance will come.

Selling is a numbers game. In baseball, three hits for ten at bats is acceptable, and even desirable. We've said it before. The same is true for selling. You're not likely to get 'em all. But then again, you're not likely to lose 'em all either. But you do have to keep going up to bat.

Natural Breaks

It is sometimes natural for a buyer to want to take a break between the interview and responding presentation phases. Before you go into a presentation phase, the buyer may want or request another appointment, another meeting. In addition, the seller—you—may want to break after the interview and before the responding presentation. Maybe during the interview, certain needs and wants surfaced that you are not adequately prepared to meet. Make up a reasonable excuse to meet again, at a later date, when you are prepared and can effectively respond.

The important point about breaks in the process is that it is most natural for the buyer to want to break *after* the responding presentation and *before* the conclusion. But you don't want him to defer his decision. Your efforts should be directed at keeping the responding presentation and the natural conclusion together.

FEES AND DISCOUNTS

There are a few basic tenents regarding fees, pricing, and discounts that apply to products and services ranging from the inexpensive to the incredible.

1. Fees and prices are irrelevant as long as they're competitive. People buy for emotional reasons—likeability, trust, rapport, perceived value, and confidence. A 10-15 percent price differential is almost never the reason buyers buy from someone else. The real reason is because the other person did a better job of selling.

2. It's generally better to be a little high than a little low. Some buyers think, "If it's a little higher, it must be better." This applies to services (attorneys, physicians, etc.) and products (cars, liquor, etc.).

3. Avoid discounts, or legitimize them. Don't discount for the sake of discounting. Create or invent your reasons for the discounts— ones that will make sense to the buyer. By the same token, if your price or fee is much higher than the competition, legitimize that too. Have reasons and tell your reasons.

4. And for marketers and sellers of services—get downpayments or cash advances, which usually are nonrefundable. Cause a buyer to commit further than a "yes." Cause him to set his schedule—prepare for change, to do something more than agree. Because you're often an intangible benefit, it is easy to sometimes hold your payment in abeyance.

SUMMARY

The natural conclusion should be a part of, not apart from, the responding presentation. Aptly named, it is a natural, mutual favorable action or commitment to buy. Have and display an attitude of assumptiveness about closing. Scoring is easy when you touch all the bases—including home plate. And it would be unnatural not to close! Although natural breaks in the selling process may occur, either at your initiation or the buyer's, avoid breaking between the responding presentation and natural conclusion. Time and space between these two steps is critical. And the more time that passes, the greater the chance for a missed sale.

Summarize the needs and wants for the buyer along with the agreements and concurrences reached during previous steps in the process. Your summaries confirm, reinforce, and substantiate an assumptiveness in your closing question or statement.

Have alternative closes or choices in mind—give the buyer a choice of two things. Buyers like to buy, they don't like to be sold. Help them realize it's their decision. If they say, "no," adapt and reinterview. Stay in the batter's box. Stay close.

Your fees should be competitive or higher. Don't use discounts unless (1) it's the only way to win and (2) you can make it appear legitimate.

The natural conclusion is the last of the four steps in a track to run on.

In order to give some idea of the number of minutes one might normally spend in a one-hour selling presentation that attempts to stay on the track, here are some guidelines, based on what I've experienced most often. The most important elements are italicized.

(3-5 minutes)   I. OPENING: Your purpose is to establish the value
                 of yourself, the moment, or the topic. Accom-

plished with presence (dress, bearing, eye contact, nonverbal comments, and so on) and with the opening statement (pique curiosity, offer a benefit, and so on).

(30-45 minutes)   II. INTERVIEW: Ask to ask general and open-ended questions about specific needs or wants. Discuss and elaborate on them. Be empathetic—what's important here is your buyer's wants, needs, goals, concerns, and so on.

(10-15 minutes)   III. RESPONDING PRESENTATION: *Provide specific solutions* to needs and wants that surfaced in the interview. Respond to the buyer's emotions and support your response with logic. Offer evidence that supports your claims. Gain concurrence and agreements with your response.

(1 minute)   IV. NATURAL CONCLUSION: A *question or statement* that evokes a favorable action or commitment.

Here's how a one-hour long sales presentation ought to look in outline form. The three most important elements of the entire dialogue are italicized.

The *opening* is not the most important part of the selling presentation but not having a good one is a sin of omission. Not having a good one is missing a good opportunity to set up the hour to make it work well and in your favor.

The *interview* is the most important part and the key is to get to the needs and wants. Get them clearly and specifically discussed. The buyer should be led to feeling strongly about these. The focus is almost totally on the buyer, his firm, situation, and so on. Do not proceed further until you are satisfied with your findings regarding needs and wants.

The *responding presentation* is when (and only when) the seller comes into focus as the provider, the source, and so on. *Remember, the degree to which the seller has gotten the buyer to be specific about needs and wants now equates to the degree to which the seller can be specific in his response, treatment, recommendation*, and so on. Frequently there is a back and fourth motion from Interview to Responding Presentation, i.e., buyers ask question and seller responds, seller asks question and buyer responds, etc. The key here is to stay here continuing this process until both buyer and seller are convinced of the specific need or want and solutions—and not go on to the natural conclusion until the seller is convinced.

The *natural mutual conclusion* should now be almost as easy as a skillful surgeon's scalpel. Swift, appropriate, and clean.

Retaining
Clients
and Customers

Assuming a favorable action or commitment on the part of the buyer, a carefully planned and executed client retention effort must be made on your part. The key to success when marketing and selling products, services, and ideas rests in the amount of repeat business any individual or firm enjoys. This is true for two reasons.

1. Retained clients and customers are for the most part satisfied clients and customers.
2. Satisfied clients and customers can most often be your best source for new business.

Retaining clients is more than just making business associates out of people. It's that plus some!

Client retention is achieved through several factors.

1. Providing high-quality and timely service.
2. Recognizing client retention as part of the overall marketing process.
3. Becoming a friend, counselor, confidant, sounding board—more than merely a service provider.

Of extreme importance to retaining clients, is the necessity for you to become more than a business associate. One of the keys to retaining clients is establishing a relationship with the buyer, or with individuals who are decision makers, so that no one else would be considered to provide a service similar to your own. Even when a different service is called for, you should have a word in the decision. Expanding or extending your existing service, or even a new one, to the satisfied client is usually the easiest and surest kind of sale, as opposed to dealing with new clients and/or new services.

CLIENT RETENTION EXERCISE

Complete this exercise to determine your current level of client retention. The exercise is a kind of score card to show you how you are presently doing with one of your clients.

Write the name of your second most important client, the one who provides you with the second highest amount of business, in the upper left hand corner in Column 1. Beneath the name of your second most important client, write the name of the chairman of the board, the president, or the proprietor. Beneath that person's name, in the same column, write the names of the key people associated with that firm or organization. At the bottom of the column, total the number of names you listed. It is possible to number a dozen people and more when you consider board members, the firm's attorney, banker, and so on.

In the second column at the top of the chart, write what each of the people you listed in Column 1 call you. At the bottom of Column 2, add up the total number of times you are called by your first name. If there is a significant difference between the number at the bottom of Column 1 and Column 2—look out! You may be lacking sufficient closeness.

The next column, Column 3, is where you indicate how many times you've had one-on-one contact (not phone calls or letters) with each of the people you listed in Column 1, on either business or nonbusiness matters. Go down the column and add up the total number of personal, one-on-one contacts you've had with the list of names during the past twelve months.

If your number is about the same as the number of people listed in Column 1, you may not be sufficiently close.

CLIENT RETENTION EXERCISE

	Column 1 *Names*	*Column 2* *Labels*	*Column 3* *One-on-One Contacts* *in the Last Year*
1.			
2.			
3.			
4.			
5.			
6.			
7.			
8.			
9.			
10.			
Totals			

As far as the number of one-on-one contacts with those key people in a twelve-month period, the numbers vary greatly. The highest I've ever heard is 206. That indicates one of two things. Either there are a lot of problems and you are putting out fires every day, or you are close. If you're that close to the buyer, the relationship is not in jeopardy.

Supposing the number is eight. In a year's time you are seeing all of these key people only eight times. That's a problem. You are inviting vulnerability.

There is an old saying that birds of a feather flock together. It's true. Financial people tend to relate to financial people. Consulting people tend to consult with whomever it is that hired them. The message here is "get to know the C.E.O.," the decision makers: Get close, and *stay close.*

Too many times we get close to the wrong people. The chief operating officer, the president, the chairman, the proprietor, and the principals are the people who make the decisions. Those are the people to whom you want to get close and stay close.

GETTING AND STAYING CLOSE

How can we, in fact, get close to and stay close to our clients? I've defined client retention as having four elements:

1. Setting a proper and ethical standard in personal and professional behavior. This invokes the transfer rule. Your conduct, manner, and attitudes in nonbusiness activities is usually subconsciously perceived by the buyer as a reflection of how technically competent you are or what kind of an effort you give his or her account. You've got to set an example, not in just the way you are dressed, but in your language, your deportment, and your general conduct.

Sometimes a golf ball rolls under a bush and we just pull it out a few inches so we can take a decent swing at it. I say they transfer that act to the kind of seminar leader, or consultant you are. Maybe it's unfair and maybe it's unrelatable. If there is no linkage intellectually, there is one emotionally.

You have one drink too many and make a foul statement. Again, intellectually there is no linkage, but emotionally there is. If you can speak as an expert in the field of politics or whatever, people emotionally transfer that to what kind of businessman or what kind of an accountant you are. You have an obligation to conduct yourself in a way that is easy to relate to and respectable.

2. If you want to retain your clients—study them. And study the industry. Know the man, the firm, and the industry. There is never a substitute for knowing what you are dealing with, for doing your homework!

3. You must become conversationally capable on topics that have nothing to do with the subject at hand, on things that are at a higher level than the weather or sports. I'm talking about things like fine wines, music, art, and so on. There are some people that you can engage for a period of time on fine wines and as a result of that, they will see you as a better or more knowledgeable and sophisticated person overall. If you want to retain a client you'd better have several areas with which you can relate in order to make a client feel like more than just a business associate.

4. I cannot emphasize the importance of making yourself easy to talk to. If you are the kind of person who is, in fact, easy to talk to you are ahead of the game. But also, because you are out of a client's mainstream of activity you are a breath of fresh air. Remember:

- Be still—physically and mentally—with the client.
- Be close physically and accessible. You're there to help.
- Usually it's useful to hold back evaluations and let the client "pour it all out." Just respond by saying, "Yes, I see, I understand, go on." You are, of course, ultimately paid to give evaluations and advice, but occasionally it helps just to be there so he can unload. Typically, he can't do so with his own vice president.

SAYING "THANKS"

There is another important consideration with respect to retaining clients. It is your willingness to say, "thanks." We often fail to express appreciation for being able to serve the client. When we are selling, when we are going through this process, we put our best foot forward. We put on ties and suits and we really try to impress the client with a lot of wonderful things. It's like *courting*. We give them our best shot. What happens ten years later? Frequently, the aftersales service gets a little sloppy. Complacency sets in. We don't put out the best that we are capable of putting out.

You should express appreciation to your clients, tell them you really are happy to serve them. Even a hand-written note that says, "You are the kind of person I really like doing business with" will accomplish this goal. We don't do that often enough.

I had a very interesting experience awhile back. I went to the King Tut exhibit in Los Angeles without tickets. I approached people asking if anyone had extra tickets. This went on for three or four minutes. Then luckily, I saw a friend and I said, "Gus! How are you?" We shook hands and he said, "Are you going to the exhibit?" I told him I didn't have any tickets. He said, "Let me try something, just a second."

He went away for five minutes and then came back and said, "Here's your tickets." And he wouldn't let me pay for them. Two days later I wrote him a note and said, "I really appreciate what you did. It was good seeing you again, and by the way, here's a book. You will like it because you are one of these." The book was entitled *The Greatest Salesman in the World.* He called me back and said that was the greatest thing in the world. And if anybody ever asks him what he thinks of me and my services, he is going to give me more than just a good referral.

I don't think we remember quite often enough to thank people. Expressing appreciation is a necessary element of the entire marketing and selling process—especially client retention. Consider sending a personal note of thanks, a book, or arranging a meeting for the purpose of expressing appreciation.

SIMPLE STRATEGIES

Here are some common sense simple strategies for retaining clients:

1. Send copies of key documents you produce.
2. When you work on your client's case during the evening or on a weekend, design a method of letting him know you were "thinking" about him beyond the 9-5 routine.
3. Return your client's calls promptly and answer any letters or correspondence promptly.
4. Send copies of key incoming documents you receive.
5. Make in-person visits. Visit clients at their place of business.

The emphasis is being "in sight" and "in mind."

Finally, there are three kinds of people you can do business with.

1. The people that you know and like, and who know and like you.
2. The people that perhaps you don't like or care for, and they don't care for you.
3. All the rest of the people in the world.

Which of the three would you rather deal with? Obviously, people that you know and they know you. If you do a good job of client retention you'll get a whole lot more business. You can get most of the new business you want from existing clientele if you treat them right.

Refer again to the marketing telescope. Good client retention feeds the front of the telescope, providing you with new leads, referrals, and new opportunities for business. Recognizing, and doing something about the fact that client retention is a part of the overall marketing process is the fourth key element in what client retention is all about.

You should take a "preventive medicine" approach to ongoing business. Most people have a physical examination once a year. You have to do the same thing with your clients/customers. Once a year you should be saying to major clients, "The meter is off. I'd like to know how you feel about what I am doing with you. I'd like to know what you think about the services I have provided within the last year. Are there some things you think we ought to be doing, or some things we are not doing as well as you'd like?"

If they say, "Well, I didn't think as of September you were doing up to your normal standards," you want to know that! Furthermore, if the intent is to retain the client you will know what he is happy with and what he isn't happy with. The annual checkup, the preventive medicine element of client retention, is critical.

SUMMARY

Here are the Ten Commandments of Good Business Practice. They apply to you and your client/customer.

1. The client is the most important person in any business.
2. The client is not dependent upon you, rather you are dependent upon the client.
3. The client is not an interruption of your work, rather he is the purpose of your work.
4. The client does you a favor when he calls, you are not doing him a favor by serving him.
5. The client is a part of your business. If you were to sell your business you would include the client in it.
6. The client is not a cold statistic, he is a flesh and blood human being of feeling and emotion, like you.

7. The client is not someone to argue with or to match wits with.

8. The client is a person who brings you his wants or needs—it is your job to fill them.

9. The client deserves the most courteous and attentive treatment you can give him.

10. The client is the lifeblood of your business.

A TREK THROUGH THE TELESCOPE

We have completed our look at the Four Phases of marketing and selling yourselves, your ideas, your products and services. In this chapter, we are going to follow an actual case study through the Four Phases. The names and certain points have been changed for the purpose of the case study.

Phase I

Sam, a young professional consultant in a medium-sized energy consulting firm, joins an association of engineers, scientists, and administrators called the National Alliance for the Constructive Use of Energy (NACUE). The group meets monthly for dinner and offers a speaker on energy-related topics. Sam's purpose in joining the organization is twofold: (1) it is his area of expertise; it is his discipline and favorite subject, and (2) it is a chance to meet more people in the field, hear about new projects, and possibly create additional business.

Sam is favorably impressed with the quality of people and the meeting. All new members and nonmember guests are asked to introduce themselves and offer a little of their background. Sam ends the night with a drink with an acquaintance he made during the meeting. The next month's meeting of NACUE turns out to be the semiannual business meeting. One of the committees needs a small, one-time job that is right up Sam's alley. He volunteers. Sam agrees to get a summary report to the chairman before the next meeting.

Sam mentions this to his supervisor at work who in turn, recommends a different report that would be even better. Sam agrees and sends both reports to the committee chairman of NACUE two weeks before his project is due. At the next monthly meeting, Sam's reports are discussed. However, the evening's guest speaker, Joe, attacks the reports as biased and incomplete. Sam asks a question that is very difficult for Joe to handle. After the meeting, Sam, Joe, and several others gather in the bar and talk late into the night about the pros and cons of various people's positions.

Three months and three meetings later, Sam is asked if he would agree to be vice chairman of a committee. He agrees to do so. Meanwhile, Sam's boss is in New York and attends a national convention of public utility administrators. Joe, who had criticized Sam's reports, is on the agenda. He and Sam's boss meet and laugh about Sam's remarks at the earlier meeting. Later, Joe asks if Sam's boss would be available for a panel discussion in the spring in Chicago.

When spring rolls around, Sam's boss is too busy to attend the Chicago meeting. He asks Sam to take over for him. Sam is delighted and his boss makes arrangements with the sponsoring organization to have Sam take his place. Because the panel discussion is a different and stimulating experience, Sam prepares extremely well. During the meeting, Sam finds himself very much in agreement with Joe, the same person with whom he had crossed swords almost a year before.

As a result of this encounter, Sam and Joe have dinner, and Joe reveals he is leaving his company because of poor management and poor planning. Sam is interested in the job because his background is in the financial management of utilities. After a long night, Sam returns home full of data about Joe's company. He asks his boss and others in his firm if they know someone in Joe's firm, but has no luck. Sam decides to call to ask if Joe minds if he contacts Joe's company president, Mr. Young. Joe says, "Sure." When Sam phones Mr. Young is not interested in talking to him. Sam gets busy on a large project and puts contacting the president on the back burner. He does, however, send a brochure following his phone conversation and two articles over the next year.

The following year, Sam is chairman of the Public Information Committee of NACUE. As such, he is asked by a midwestern utility company to speak to a regional governmental agency. Present at this meeting is Joe's former boss, Mr. Young, who is president of the host utility firm. Sam's speech strikes a nerve with several utility executives, including Mr. Young. The local newspaper quotes from Sam's speech. One of Mr. Young's subordinates shows him the article. That night in the hotel, Sam reads that Mr. Young was in the audience and remembers his futile effort to contact him by phone a year ago. At breakfast the next morning, Sam sees Joe, who is now consulting with Mr. Young's company, and asks if Joe can help Sam get an introduction to Mr. Young. Joe agrees to do it in his own way.

Joe suggests to the vice president of finance, "Sam is one man who can help guide your troubled firm out of its financial and legislated doldrums." The vice president is very eager for this help. Armed with the newspaper article quoting Sam, the vice president tells Mr. Young about him. Mr. Young is now aware of Sam's growing reputation and agrees to a meeting.

All of the above occurred in the first phase of marketing—creating a public image. Sam joined a professional organization, became an activist (transfer rule), made a speech, utilized brochures and articles, was quoted in the newspaper, and so on. The time factor here is about eighteen months.

Phase II

The meeting between Mr. Young and Sam is not a meeting at all, but a handshake and a short conversation. During the conversation, both Sam and Mr. Young are pushed for time. However, Sam now realizes how much he can help Mr. Young's company because he has read its published financial reports and inquired about its track record. But Mr. Young seems cool and not eager to pursue things further. Sam has also learned that Mr. Young is a close friend of one of his boss's clients. Sam's boss agrees with Sam to try to get his client to put in a good word for their company and Sam in particular. The client agrees to help and asks how to help? Sam's boss says a letter would be excellent, and even agrees to send his client a rough draft. A week later, the client calls back, talks to Sam and his boss, and says he's sending the letter off that day. "Good luck, glad I could help," he says.

The letter showed that a copy went to Sam, so Mr. Young knows Sam is aware of it. By now he's surrounded by positive inputs regarding Sam and his work. When Sam calls, he is cordial and asks if he is going to the NACUE's annual Legislative Meeting in Washington, D.C. in two months. Sam says yes, and Mr. Young invites him to join his table at the president's dinner. Sam agrees.

The president's dinner is lavish, and there are too many people present to get close to Mr. Young. Sam's wife is seated fairly near Mrs. Young. Sam is off at the other end of the table. Mrs. Young reveals that Mr. Young is a golf fanatic and is eager to get in a round while he's in D.C. Sam shoots a pretty good round himself.

Sam calls his boss and asks if he can contact his friend, a congressman's aid, to see if he can arrange for a foursome at Olympic—

the prestigious course where many legislators play. Sam's boss and the aid come through the next day for a 1:10 tee-off.

Sam calls Mr. Young and says he's got the time and place. Would he and a friend like to join Sam and a friend? Mr. Young is delighted and accepts. Sam then finds a friend to play with him.

The setting and the weather are beautiful. The foursome plays and has a great outing—but no business talk. Then they retire to the "19th hole" for a drink.

Mr. Young is thoroughly pleased with the day, his game and the outing. He is warming up to Sam. Sam decides to ask Mr. Young for some advice about universities with offerings on nuclear energy. Mr. Young, who is a board member of the University of Michigan, suggests *three* schools *only* in the nation and gives reasons why. As they part, Mr. Young suggests they have a meeting to discuss what Sam might be able "to bring to our company." Sam says he'll call for an appointment.

Four days later, Sam calls Mr. Young and reveals he has contacted one of the three schools Mr. Young suggested. Sure enough, the school had exactly what Sam and his company needed for some continuing training and development. Sam thanked Mr. Young, who was most pleased at this information. He asks if Sam could meet with him and his vice president of operations. Sam agrees and sets an appointment the following week.

All of Phase II could be called "Developing relationships." Sam did his homework, got third party support, sought advice and counsel, and demonstrated resourcefulness and assertiveness. He moved from a contact with Mr. Young to "buyer interest."

Phase III

Now, Sam goes to work. He calls Joe for information on his old firm, particularly about changes in personnel, looks up information on Mr. Young's firm, and plans his approach. Joe says the current vice president is heavy in engineering and Mr. Young's background is general administration—there is nobody who is strong in finance. That is the real problem he tells Sam. Sam is fairly certain this is right, based on his observations. Sam prepares his presentation and written documentation. He is ready.

Mr. Young is warm and receptive to Sam. He says he has done his homework on Sam and that Indiana Gas & Electric had great things to say about what Sam and his firm had accomplished there less than one year ago. Sam's response is, "I'm delighted to hear that. Who did you speak to there, George Evans? Tell me what George had to say."

The ensuing presentation and interview goes smoothly, and lasts ninety minutes. But when Sam suggests a specific course of action, Mr. Young says he'd like to think about it. Sam suggests they take a certain smaller action now and consider the major move later based on some preliminary findings. "Not for now," says Mr. Young. Sam agrees to be in touch, with another idea, in a few days. They part warmly.

Sam gets on the phone to George Evans at Indiana Gas & Electric and thanks him for the boost. Then Sam asks if George knows anything about Mr. Young and the vice president. George says Mr. Young is totally hamstrung by a board of directors, "None of whom are qualified to be on the board—but don't quote me." Now Sam knows he can help Mr. Young.

He calls back with a new approach, very eager to talk to Mr. Young alone. Mr. Young is curious but willing. Sam arrives two days later and explains how he can help Mr. Young by doing a one-week financial feasibility program to shed light on a new source of revenue. He and perhaps his board of directors might find it most helpful, he says. Mr. Young agrees to the study.

Phase III was typical of what happens during the selling phase. Sam makes a quick response, carefully plans his strategy, contacts contacts, plans the presentation, gets agreement, favorable action, or commitment, and follows up quickly.

Phase IV

Scene: Two years and $400,000 worth of business later.

Sam and Mr. Young (whom he now calls "Charles") are having lunch and reviewing what was accomplished in the last project Sam worked on for Mr. Young. Sam is determining from Charles what parts helped most, least, what Charles understood, what he didn't quite grasp and so on. Charles remarks about how much more time he has now, and Sam challenges him to a golf "championship." One area of concern for Charles is a part of Sam's work which threatens his vice president of finance. Sam should tread lightly with him, he says. Sam expresses concern and says he'll do what he can to straighten that out.

After the meeting, Sam calls the vice president of finance and asks if he can see him, but he's too busy. Sam leaves for home, but writes the vice president a hand-written note asking for a meeting. Four days later, Sam calls and arranges to see the vice president at a NACUE regional meeting. Unknown to the vice president, Sam arranges to have the two of them at the president's table. The vice president is flattered when he learns of this and Sam senses a softening in his attitude. Sam asks the vice president to help him get to another noncompeting company in the same geographical region. The vice president agrees and the rest of the evening is cordial.

Sam writes the vice president a note the following week expressing thanks for the help. The vice president makes the contact and informs Sam. Sam sends Charles a note expressing his appreciation for the help and fine work of the vice president. The vice president is called into Mr. Young's office and congratulated for his efforts.

At Christmas, Sam sends Charles a funny card about golf and reminds him of their upcoming spring golf outing. He also sends the vice president an article with a personal note implying the vice president may be the one person in the firm who understands the subtle and long-term influence of the article. A week later he calls and they discuss the article. Sam suggests the two of them consider a company response to the publisher.

Part IV reflects some of the ways to retain clients. Use preventive medicine—take the client's temperature, become more than a business associate, make a hero of someone in the client's firm, and so on. Of course, doing the job you were paid to do and a little more is important—but as a professional that's a given.

This has been a typical trek through the telescope—a progression through the Four Phases of marketing by a professional skilled in marketing and selling.

THE MOST
IMPORTANT GAME:
YOU

10

Setting Your Marketing and Selling Goals

For over twenty years I have studied why people are effective. I've participated in dozens of seminars on effective human behavior, and I've taught hundreds of seminars on such topics as communications, decision making, self-image psychology, and goal setting. I have concluded there is a combination of three very important and universal elements present in all successful people: *Knowledge, commitment, and a healthy self-image*.

Knowledge is acquired skills and techniques, education in formal and informal settings, personal experiences, and on-the-job training. It is the sum total of bits of data acquired and used over a lifetime. It is the learning and understanding of procedures, methods, and means of movement, growth, and change. Sometimes it is the result of just plain hard work.

Knowledge could be referred to as homework. And there is no substitute for doing your homework. One of the key results of doing one's homework is learning what we want, what will gratify us, what directions we should take—in a word, our goals.

Commitment is related to one's desire to accomplish; it is the values we perceive in doing whatever we're doing. Commitment is a resolve to extend ourselves. It is a degree of willingness to achieve. Self image is so critical to your success and effectiveness that the last three chapters of the book are devoted to that topic. In the first two parts of this book I have offered information about sales and marketing methods that have proven effective for me. And based upon hundreds of hours of teaching, training, and drilling others, I know these ideas and procedures have proven successful for thousands of others. Naturally, my hope is you will use these ideas also, but it is critically important that you know what *you* want. All the knowledge in the world is useless if you don't use it. The most important game is you and knowing what you want to accomplish.

Let's start with a fresh look at your self and your goals. It's important for you to set not only some sales and marketing objectives, but business, career, and life goals. What do you want to grow to? A larger firm? A different kind of company? Toward another discipline? More income? Higher sales? A change of personal or professional lifestyle? No matter what fits you, you'll do so by (a) working harder and smarter, and (b) improving your self-image. These are the two ways in which the human system generates growth and change.

Dreams make plans come true, but the reverse seldom works. The following rarely, if ever, happens: Here we are at some given point (x). Let's save our money, schedule our time, arrange for baby/house sitting, conduct some study and research (all of which is a plan of action), and finally, "Where shall we go?"

People get very little accomplished in that manner, instead for example, a friend returns from Europe with beautiful photos, remarkable tales of adventure and history, and mementos. You catch the bug and decide to spend three months in Europe. It will still take a good plan of action but the dream is what will cause the development of an action plan, not the reverse.

There is an old story that goes like this: A man approaches a ticket agent at a railroad station and asks to buy a ticket. "To where?" asks the agent. The man replies, "Oh, it doesn't make a lot of difference, anywhere will do." The perplexed agent replies, "I can't sell you a ticket unless I know where you want to go!" The man replies, "Just sell me a ticket to somewhere, I don't care where to." The agent frowned and said, "One way or round trip?" The man replied, "Round trip." The agent said, "To where?" The man simply replied, "Back here!"

This story is ridiculous, but perhaps applicable. What do you want your company to do for you? What kind of a business/practice gratifies you the most? The makeup, size, location, ownership, and so on, are all important. You must clarify the answers to these questions. Can you honestly describe your desired business/practice? Can you pinpoint its characteristics, purposes, or wanted results?

The following are some guidelines for you to use in your goal-setting process. There are seven parts to consider.

1. *Assessment.* I hope you will be prompted to pinpoint and clarify your business/practice, and what you want your business to do for you in the exercise later in this chapter.

2. *Yours or someone else's?* Are you working toward pleasing your parents? Only your company and not you? Your spouse and not yourself. Society (good luck)? It is your ideas and services, and yourself that is being marketed and sold here—*your* toil, *your* energy, *your* creativity—you'd better satisfy, even gratify, yourself in your endeavors.

3. *Are Your Goals Aligned With Those Who Count?* Who counts? Your spouse, firm, boss, accountant, attorney, lawyer, banker, a fellow partner—all told perhaps a dozen people. (The rest of the world is not overly impressed, concerned, or even interested in your progress toward achievement of your goals.) You will profit and smoothen the path if you will share, modify, create, and build enthusiasm, in those few people who count. This presupposes you want to satisfy the needs and wants of customers and clients. This, of course, needs to be done but I am not treating these people as part of your inner circle or team.

4. *Alignment.* Here is an important and applicable analogy. Imagine I have in my hands two bars of metal. One is a magnet and one is not. They are composed of the same chemical ingredients. The only difference is the molecules in the plain bar are nonaligned (or at random). The molecules in the magnet are aligned in a to-and-fro fashion that creates an additional thrust which is missing in the other bar. This alignment in a business or practice is the cause of synergism. One plus one no longer equals 2, but 3, 4 and more. You have every reason to align yourself with those key people in your life and work toward your mutual growth and well-being.

5. You should get goals *far enough* "out there" to cause you to reach, extend yourself, be creative, and energetic but *not so far* that they are out of sight, vague, nebulous, and unproductive. Your goals should be used on a daily basis as regulators or guidelines. Goals set and then set aside produce little if anything. Instead you must remind yourself regularly of where you are going and why.

6. *Goals clearly defined in writing* are more useful than those

we keep in our heads for two reasons. Writing clarifies and specifies. It is sometimes easy, sometimes tough to put what we want on paper. Secondly, there is an element of commitment when we write things down. The more we commit ourselves to any goal, the more likely we are to achieve it.

7. We need to *reassess our goals* and plans at least once a year to correct, and further evaluate the appropriateness of them, or re-commit.

The guidelines are based on the assumption you want your business/ practice to grow in some way. To the degree this has geniune importance to you, you are about to experience a catalytic happening. Whenever any human system decides it genuinely wants something of real value, two things happen: We become more creative and we become more energetic.

Dr. Victor Frankl, a Jewish-Austrian psychiatrist, was caught in the German prison camps in Aushwitz and Dachau. He experienced torture, starvation, deprivation, and humiliation. He wrote a book about his experience in those camps called, *Man's Search for Meaning.* His main theme is, people who have a purpose in life, a mission, a reason to live (goals) live—people who don't—don't! He even observed both in a single person several times.

A man who had endured all of those excruciating difficulties for months would receive the word that his wife was executed or his village wiped out, would turn a mental switch, give up, and die within two weeks. The reverse of this principle is also true, and applies to selling and marketing as much or more than any activity in life. The following is a true story about this principle.

Gene is a computer programmer and analyst. His background, training, and education is highly technical. The idea of working for others, expending huge amounts of energy, and receiving a weekly salary was becoming less and less appealing to him. He wanted to become a consultant to others, and own his own business.

The more he thought about his situation, the less attractive it became and the more he focused on what he thought he'd really enjoy. Gene attended a seminar I conducted and refocused his professional life. He decided he definitely wanted to make a change, wrote down some business and marketing goals, and began to use them. I could see Gene could really taste having his own business.

With his training and experience in the aerospace industry, Gene had all the tools needed to perform valuable services for customers. And yet, he still needed two things.

He needed to hone in on specific long-range and short-range goals, and he also needed to sell and market himself. Gene started the growth pattern by working more hours than anyone I've ever seen—usually 60-75 hours a week—about 50 hours on his employer's time and the rest for himself. He wrote letters, made personal calls, got his wife to help him, recontacted former associates, and finally concluded he was about 50 percent ready to move out on his own. He lined up several projects that paid him a small to medium fee. The last step was the *coup de grace*. Gene proposed to his employers that they use his services as an outside consultant at a fraction of the cost of his salary. They could save money, get the knowledge he possessed now, and the additional expertise he would accumulate from work in other firms.

Gene's employers jumped at the idea because they were looking for opportunities to advance people Gene had trained. This represented the other 40 percent of work Gene determined he needed to start. He was willing to gamble on generating the additional business, and so he struck out on his own. His energy and creativity are now 100 percent focused on his own enterprise, his goals, what his company can do for him (and what his company can do for others).

This process was approximately eighteen months from apparent seed to fruition. I point out this true story to emphasize that when you decide what's important to you and go after it, you develop additional creativity and higher energy levels.

If you take these principles and point them at selling yourself, your ideas, and your services you clearly need to know what you want in terms of a short-term tactic—a sales presentation—when you walk out of that meeting, what favorable action or commitment do you want to have caused?

In marketing—a longer range strategy—what are the objectives of your efforts, what influences do you want them to have on this year's business? And finally, what do you want this business/practice to do for you, your career, and your lifestyle? The degree to which your selling and marketing goals are clear and well-defined, the easier they will be to accomplish. So give careful consideration to the following goal-setting exercise.

GOAL-SETTING PROCESS

I. The following is how I want my business/practice to be in one year (or two years or five years):

   1. Specialize in: _____

   _____

   2. Size: _____

   _____

   3. Sales Volume: _____

   _____

   4. Key Accomplishments: _____

   _____

II. My long-range strategy to accomplish these goals is (elaborate on key thrusts):

   _____

   _____

   _____

   _____

   _____

   _____

   _____

   _____

   _____

III. Three of my most important short-range goals and tactics to accomplish them are:

   1. _____

   _____

   _____

   _____

2. _____

_____

_____

_____

3. _____

_____

_____

_____

IV. Key people I need to persuade or influence to help achieve these long-range and/or short-range goals:

_____

_____

_____

_____

_____

THE SET OF THE SAIL

To conclude this chapter I want to relate a brief story that has had meaning for me over the years. It is about a man who tried land sailing for the first time in his life. A friend told him a few of the basics—how to catch the wind in his sail, which way to lean, and so on. The man caught on quickly and was soon racing across the open spaces, his sail full of the wind.

Suddenly the man was caught completely off guard as another racer approached—coming directly at him—with full sail. The man couldn't understand how this could happen! How could both race along in opposite directions?

The message is simple but worth repeating: "It's not the forces of nature that dictate your course in life. It is how you set your sail."

I hope this exercise helps you to begin setting your sail. You need to hone in on what you want to accomplish with your marketing and selling goals.

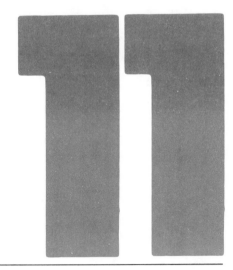

The
Self-Image

Every good marketer and seller I've ever known or observed possessed a positive and healthy self-image as sellers and marketers. They felt at home, natural, and at ease with persuasion and leadership. Why this common denominator called a self-image?

First let me define self-image. It is a subconscious conclusion or truth about oneself in any area—sports, public speaking, sales, making friends, management, or supervising one's own accomplishments. Everyone has these "truths." They are a result of years of conditioning and one's values. Take the young person with a paper route who was required to make monthly collections and serve customers. To the degree it became easy and natural, even fun, that youngster began to develop an image of himself as a salesperson, an entrepreneur. Such an attitude might develop further as he became involved in "spirit week," the Debate Club, or student body politics in high school. In college the same young man would likely be attracted to similar activities on a larger or higher scale, and other people-oriented activities. Is it any wonder by age 22 or 23 the person is interested in and attracted to sales or marketing? They're quite at home with it, they have developed a self-image of people orientation, inner action, and social ability. They have, beneath the surface of conscious thought, a "truth" about being able to meet, engage, and persuade others.

These fully developed self-images literally control our lives. They act as spigots. They allow us to use our knowledge, skills, data, techniques, and experiences in sales—or any field. How we use them depends on whether they are positive or negative. Of course, a good self-image alone, unsupported by education (formal or informal) experience, knowledge, and so on, will render an individual ineffective.

It should also be pointed out that the self-image is not public imagery, or what we want the marketplace to perceive. We dealt with that earlier. Rather, your self-image is the gut-level truth you honestly feel about yourself. "The real me," as it relates to sales, retaining clients, closing, meeting new people, and writing articles.

In addition to acting like a spigot the self-image can also be likened to the cruise control on an automobile.

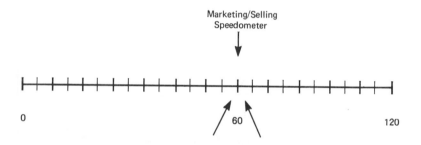

Just as a car's cruise control prevents it from traveling at a speed much above or below a predetermined setting, an individual's self-image prevents him from behaving above or below a certain behavior range. This includes how frequently we solicit business, the volume of annual business we generate, our number of clients, our kind of customers, our income range or level, and our savings, investments, and net worth. All of these are directly controlled by the awesome influence of our self-image.

The primary difference between someone who sells $30,000 and someone who sells $300,000 is mainly in their respective self-images, not in their expertise and techniques. The techniques used are likely to be very similar! Not so in self images. Only one sees himself as a big hitter. Only one is perfectly comfortable and natural dealing with big numbers, and interacting with those who have wealth and great influence.

The comfort range translates to our performance or our environmental circumstances in life. Our comfort range is regulated by our self-image just like the cruise control is regulated by electronic circuitry. The comfort range includes the client or customer responsibility load we feel right and natural with, the level of management

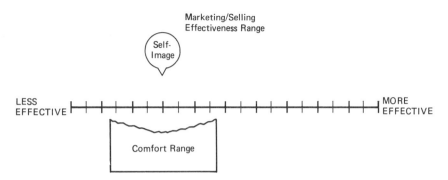

people in a business with whom we are able to best relate, the range of earnings we expect, the degree to which we feel capable of making speeches, even the ease with which we handle "nos" in selling situations. There is a continuing relationship between the self-image and the comfort range. We simply do not have a strong, positive self-image and perform poorly on any consistent basis. Neither do we know deeply that we are quite ineffective in a given activity and consistently perform well in it. Further, it can be said we have a mid-range (normal performance or circumstance), an upper range (when you're hot, you're hot), or a lower range (I should've stayed in bed)—all of which are at least within the bounds of acceptability.

One of three things happens when we behave in a manner outside our comfort range—not necessarily in the following sequence or in thirds. When we start performing "over our head" in tennis, earnings, get into high level meetings, or give a speech in front of too large a crowd we are probably out of our comfort range. When we spend a night in jail, play our favorite sport very poorly, blow several sales, and so on, we are probably out of our comfort range also. In either case we will tend to do one of the following things— get back where we "belong," recreate that with which we're accustomed, or make an adjustment.

In a seminar, a 30-year-old man related this story. He made his college tennis team, but just barely. He was the eighth or ninth man on the team. The team qualified for the state tournament and he felt fortunate to make the traveling squad. Lo and behold, the first day of the tournament he was matched against the top player in the state—the top seed. My friend said he was amused, as loose as he could be and had everything to gain and nothing to lose. He went out and beat the top-seeded player 6-3 in the first set. He then began to realize the immense influence this act would have on the entire world of tennis—he had just played way over his head, and this was incredible! Crazy! He proceeded to get himself blown off the court in the next two sets, losing 6-0, 6-1.

This is not uncommon. It happens frequently in sports and in many activities. Our friend here got back to where he belonged in a hurry. He got out of his comfort range of tennis behavior. A confirming response was experienced by the top player. If he was asked at the end of the day, "How'd you play?" He likely would answer, "Not very well, as a matter of fact, some guy I never heard of actually beat me in the first set." (I played beneath my level—out of my comfort range.)

The previous example is classically illustrated by the $30,000-a-year salesman ($2,500 a month) who in the first month of the year nets himself $10,000. In the second month he , (a) gets sick, (b) goes skiing, (c) straightens out his files, and (d) starts a home improvement project. The reason? He is acting so far removed from his self-image (in real truth), that he is subconsciously getting back where he belongs. But wait, doesn't he want to earn more? It is reasonable to assume he does. However, we have a critical and universal conflict here. On one side we have a desire to earn more, on the other we have the self-image. The pivotal point is that whenever there is a conflict between desire and self-image, the self-image will always overcome the desire. It isn't that he needs more desire. It is the self-image that needs to change, modify, and grow in order for the salesman to begin selling consistently at larger volumes. The same principle effects your selling, tennis, public speaking, name remembering, or golf. This principle is originally derived from the aphorism in the Bible which reads,

> As a man thinketh in his heart,
> So is he.

A translation of the Biblical saying which I use is "As I Think I Am." We tend to use whatever knowledge, experience, skills, or techniques in accordance with how and what we've concluded about ourselves. We're comfortable when we're acting like ourselves (and thus effective) and uncomfortable when we're not acting like ourselves. The self-image more than anything else keeps us acting like ourselves. If you have concluded you are a technical sort or a whatever, but not a sales or marketing sort, you'll have trouble using the tools and methods presented earlier in this book. Further, I've mentioned one or three things likely to happen when we get out of our comfort range. The first is we get uncomfortable and subconsciously get back to "acceptable" behavior—normal, hot, or "I shoulda' stayed in bed." The second possibility is we tend to recreate whatever we've become accustomed to. That is, if we can't return to the normal behavior, the normal place in our worldy environment or circumstances in life, then we'll recreate a performance or circumstance which is similar to what we've become comfortable with before.

Recently I worked with some fast food stores. In one case, we had a store that was efficient and clean, morale was good, and the store had growing profits. The other store had poor morale, was inefficient, semi-clean, and had declining profits. In eight out of ten cases if we examine the store managers from their respective stores and put them into the opposite stores, the inevitable will happen. Both will "straighten out" their new place! The good store will tail off and the poor store will tend to pick up. The reason? Both managers will subconsciously perform in accordance to the way they have come to see themselves as managers. Let me make it clear that the poor manager, just like the $2,500-a-month salesman in the previous example, is not trying to perform poorly. On the contrary, he's attempting to perform well. It's just that the subconscious self-image is so overwhelmingly powerful that trying hard is not the answer. Once again, the ineffective manager needs to view himself in a better light. In both cases, manager and salesman, we are presuming equal experience, knowledge, skills and techniques. But even with a moderate edge in knowledge the stronger self-image will be the deciding factor.

The third possibility of what happens when you're out of your comfort range is the most important one. You adapt. If we perform on the positive side of our comfort range or exceed the range and accept the new behavior as appropriate, we begin to make genuine progress. Unfortunately, such a situation (the average salesman who gets a biggie) is frequently accepted as a fluke (i.e., the "C" student who gets an "A"; the non-artist who comes up with a good painting, and so on). However, to the degree our reaction to outstanding performances is, "Now that's more like it!" or, "Now I'm beginning if I really concentrated I'd be good at this," or, "Now I'm beginning to fulfill my real potential," then we are adapting. A change in the self-image is imminent.

All lasting progress in all fields begins with self-image. Therefore, it's imperative that you begin to adapt, to see yourself better, to learn to like selling and marketing and to get increasingly comfortable with these activities. When you do, your self-image grows. When your self-image grows, you change your comfort range.

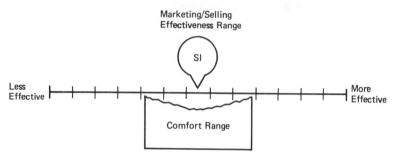

Now fluke behavior is merely hot ("That's like me!"). Formerly normal behavior is merely acceptable and what used to be acceptable behavior on the low side is no longer acceptable ("It's not like me!").

Thought Processes,
Values,
and Conditioning

In order to move ahead we sometimes have to take a short look back. This chapter explains how the mind functions and how we have developed our self-images regarding our sales willingness and ability. If we understand how any system works we can use it better and get more mileage out of it. The same applies to our thought processes. When we understand how the mind functions, we can get more out of our minds.

Although you have one mind, that mind has two levels: conscious and subconscious. What you have in your mind originated with external stimuli that your conscious mind has perceived. Yet there are limits, both physical and psychological, to the ability of the mind to take in information. Of the two limits, the psychological limits are by far the more important in determining what and how you perceive. And the two factors that are most responsible for the psychological limits are values and conditioning. Your values and conditioning are of critical importance because they are the two principal reasons you are the way you are.

Your values get in the way of your perceptions because the attention your conscious mind gives to external stimuli is in direct proportion to the value you place on those stimuli. If your primary interest is technical, you will not notice the sales opportunities as readily as you would if your highest priority was the development of new business. I know a professional man who within twenty minutes at a cocktail party will be saying, "If that's the case then we ought to be handling your account because . . ." It is second nature with him to be looking for business opportunities, and he readily picks them up. He didn't do this at age ten, fifteen, or twenty. He has learned to be this way. He has conditioned himself.

The subconscious plays a key role in how we respond to consciously perceived stimuli. It plays this role because one of its principal functions is data storage. The subconscious records and retains everything that the human system has experienced. When we perceive something, we scan our subconscious to find a meaning for the stimulus, to associate it with past experience. Once we have found an association in our subconscious, we evaluate the stimulus and make a decision to act or behave in response to the stimulus. If we have had a number of successful selling experiences we feel a bit more comfortable with the people involved, the results, and so on. The reverse is also true with negative associations.

The subconscious is truly an enormous storehouse of data. Current estimates are that the average 30-year-old person has stored in the subconscious 10 quadrillion (10,000,000,000,000,000) bits of information. You can see that you have a tremendous amount of data on which to draw, yet modern psychologists estimate that we use only one or two percent of our potential. The key, of course, is that if you see great value in business development, you will use your subconscious information far more extensively than if you are either uncomfortable with the activity or see little value in it. If you can learn to use what you know to greater advantage, you will greatly increase the use of your potential. If you are currently using only 1 percent of your potential and can increase that to 2 percent, you have experienced a 100 percent increase in the use of your potential. You can achieve that increase by getting to accept yourself as a sales and marketing type of person. One very important feature to note about the subconscious is that it accepts at face value all the data entered into it. The subconscious does not distinguish between what is good or bad, real or imagined. The subconscious does not make decisions. That is a function of the volitional conscious mind. This factor will become more meaningful in the next chapter.

REALITY AND "TRUTH"

The subconscious is also the repository of each individual's reality. Reality, in this sense, refers to all an individual's experiences and thoughts, beliefs, and attitudes about everything. This reality is what we refer to as "truth," or "how things really are" as a salesperson, a marketer, an interacter, a social being, and a question-asker. This reality has two important dimensions. First, everyone's reality is different. Reality is like a window through which we perceive external reality. But because of our conditioning, this window acts as a filter. Second, a person's reality is constantly changing as a result of new input over time.

If we "know" we have no talent as an artist, salesperson, or athlete, doing something about it can be fruitless. Those who believe they have some talent in these fields are usually the ones who tend to hone their skills. Genetic inheritance endows us with certain physical and mental characteristics that may permit us to be certain types of persons. For example, an adult man who is five feet tall has little chance of becoming an outstanding professional basketball player. Another man who is seven feet tall, *may* become one. Similarly, one person may have the "gift" of musical talent and, with training, can develop into an outstanding musician. Another person with little or no inborn musical talent probably will never become an outstanding musician. Conditioning includes all of our experiences since birth. I consider conditioning to be far more important than genetic inheritance in shaping our self-images. Numerous modern psychologists agree including Wayne Dyer, William Glasser, Joyce Brothers, and Carl Rogers.

We are all verbal creatures. We talk to ourselves all the time—up to 500 words a minute. Further, we think with pictures, concepts, imagery, dreams, and visions. Finally, we think with emotions. Words trigger images, images trigger feelings. Someone offers us an opportunity to sell, this triggers self-talk of success, eagerness, anticipation, and getting a hit, which in turn triggers pictures of meeting, developing rapport, probing, agreeing, signing, and delivering. This in turn triggers elation, satisfaction, and a sense of contribution. Once again we can reverse this when someone offers us an opportunity to sell. We self-talk ourselves about delay, ineptness, saying the wrong things, and so on, which triggers visions of smart aleck buyers, doors being closed in our faces, looking foolish, which in turn triggers discomfort, embarrassment, and rejection feelings.

THE INPUTS ARE YOURS

Although other people serve as sources of input for you, it is your self-talk—how you interpret and react to the words and actions of others, and the value you place on others and their inputs—that becomes the actual input. Thus, you create your own inputs.

You receive "positive" and "negative" inputs from many sources, including, most significantly, yourself, throughout your life. What is important is not the inputs themselves but what you do with them—whether you make them positive or negative entries to your self-image.

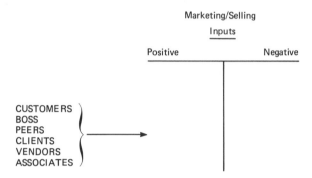

When making inputs into your self-image, you tend to reinforce whatever you consider to be valid about that self-image. Suppose, for example, that you have concluded you are a poor tennis player, but, even so, you win a tennis match. Would your self-image change? Maybe not. You might *explain* your winning by saying to yourself, "I was playing over my head," or "It was just luck." Or, you could have had a positive reaction, "Now that's more like it, maybe all my practice is starting to pay off." However, the likelihood is that you will reinforce what you know is really there about yourself: You are a poor tennis player. It isn't so much that people "bad mouth" themselves as it is that they are just "being honest."

The same thing applies to selling situations. Some people think they simply haven't got it as a salesperson. This negative self-image is constantly reinforced by additional negative inputs.

Whether you take an entry as positive or negative is also affected by your perception of the person providing the entry. It is possible, for instance, to turn a mild compliment ("That was a nice job") into a strongly positive input if you receive the compliment from a person whom you admire greatly and whose opinion you value highly. If a top salesperson whom you respect says, "You really handled that beautifully. If you wanted to sell full-time you'd put the rest of us out of business," you'd take it to heart. At the same time, you can interpret a compliment, however effusive as a negative input if you have no respect for the person offering the compliment and do not trust his or her opinions, judgments, or sincerity.

You have many self-images—employee, spouse, parent, friend, salesperson, community leader. But regardless of which self-image you are concerned with, it is important to remember three facts about self-images.

1. You gave yourself those self-images.
2. You reinforce those self-images daily.
3. What others say to you may or may not be important; what you say to yourself is *always* important.

Understanding how you developed your self-images and how you reinforce them is important because it affects your ability and willingness to grow. If you know how you get your self-images, you can, if you want to, choose to change them and grow. Growth is a decision! You decide:

- How you are going to be; the amounts of money you will earn.
- What you are going to do and how well you are going to do it.
- Where you are going to live.
- What is important to you.

Once you decide to grow, you are then living your life by design, not by default. Too many people seem not to make such decisions, and thus do not commit themselves to growth, change, effectiveness, or success. Even though your self-image has been influenced by the inputs of others and the values you place on the sources of those inputs, as well as by your early childhood conditioning, you are still the primary developer and builder of it.

Once you decide you are going to like selling and marketing and that you are going to excel at it, then you begin to live that part of your life more by design than by default.

13

Image Impression
and Affirmations

Growth occurs in two basic ways: (1) Through obtaining more sales and marketing data—by doing more "homework," preparation, and studying; by working; by getting more experience; and by practicing more and better; and (2) through the use of image impressions in which we make a directed effort at modifying our subconscious self-image as a seller and marketer.

Image impression is a technique for changing your self-image through mental rehearsal of a desired change in your behavior or circumstance. It is a process by which a person becomes mentally experienced or psychologically comfortable with an act, behavior, or circumstance before it occurs. It is related to hypnosis and similar altered mental states such as transcendental meditation, yoga, and mesmerization.

If, for example, your self-image as a public speaker is that of an inarticulate, trembling bore and you want to change that image, you can take two steps. First, collect "data," research your subject, organize your thoughts, outline your speech, and in general, prepare yourself. Second, in your mind give a fascinating, coherent, assured, and energetic presentation to an audience. Image impression, as a tool for change and growth, emphasizes the second step. The identical two processes are used in becoming an effective seller.

IDEAL VERSUS REALITY

Goethe expressed the basic concept underlying image impression most eloquently.

Treat a man as he is and he will remain so
Treat a man as he can and ought to be
And he will become as he can and ought to be.

You can paraphrase that quotation to apply to yourself.

If you treat yourself the way you are,
You will remain so.
If you treat yourself the way you can be
    and ought to be,
You will become as you can be and should be.

When you dwell on what is, you change nothing. You can neither address your potential nor change and grow. Dwelling on what is actually tends to reinforce existing behavior. However, if you dwell on what it is you want to be—focus on more ideal behavior, a more desirable image—you will tend to move in that direction.

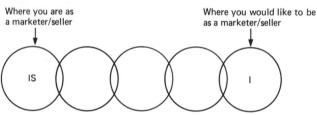

In some instances, it is necessary only to change your image of yourself to improve performance or circumstances. For example, if you think of yourself as a sloppy dresser, but decide to change that image and think of yourself as a neat, smartly attired person, you may soon find that you pay more attention to your clothes, have them cleaned and pressed more frequently, hang them up instead of dropping them in a pile on the floor, and shop for new clothing with more care. In other instances, it is also necessary to get more data—do your homework—in order to change your self-image. If you want to be a good tennis player but seldom set foot on a tennis court, you will undoubtedly need to learn and develop various aspects of the game before you can change your original self-image (poor tennis player) to a different self-image (good tennis player).

In selling, the same applies. The first two parts of this book offer "how tos" in selling and marketing. Getting up to bat and taking swings is a necessity. Now we're concerned with your concept of yourself as a hitter—hopefully, a big hitter. You need to see yourself as a big hitter in order to be one.

Redesigning Your Self-Image

Because you do not behave in conflict with your self-image on any extended basis, if you are to change you must redesign that image. Change in the self-image is a catalyst for change in behavior. If there is a conflict between your desire to change and the image you have of yourself, your image will prevail and dictate your behavior. Thus, it is your image that needs modification, and simply trying harder (having the desire to change or swing harder at the ball) does not work. Image impression is a psychologically sound process for growth because, even though you cannot erase past experiences (those are permanently stored in your nonjudgmental subconscious):

1. Only you make the entries, and
2. Your subconscious accepts whatever entries you give it and responds to those inputs.

Thus, you can redesign your self-image by consciously entering into your subconscious new, different, and more desirable imagery. When you impress on your subconscious self-image new and different imagery, you have taken an essential first step toward change and growth. This is not a matter of removing negative inputs, but rather of placing more desirable, positive inputs and images into our thought processes. You must impress upon your subconscious that which you would like it to conclude.

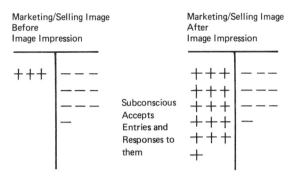

AFFIRMATIONS

Affirmation is a tool to be used in the process of image impression. An affirmation is a positive assertion, a specific means to an end. When you use an affirmation, you are impressing upon your subconscious a more ideal or desirable image, behavior, or achievement. An affirmation must be three-dimensional to correspond to the three dimensions of the thought process—self-talk, imagery, and emotion. An affirmation consists of a statement (self-talk), visualization of the scene in a positive, successful way (imagery), and experiencing the feelings in that scene (emotion). When you use affirmations, you are providing your subconscious with positive inputs. Your subconscious accepts that input, your self-image changes and grows, and your comfort range expands. The previously awesome "over my head" behavior becomes more acceptable, natural and right. The idea is to project yourself forward into the future and practice becoming adept, smooth, responsive, and comfortable in a real-life selling presentation you know you will be facing. Enter the room, greet the other person in a warm way, sense the person's receptiveness, see the room setting, start exchanging information, extract from the buyer the data you need, counsel him or her, guide him or her on the available alternatives, conclude the session by getting them to choose a best course of action, agree on details, shake hands, and feel pleased at what you've accomplished. Allow yourself to feel equal, to feel like a counselor or a teacher. Give the buyer credit for being an effective manager, owner, or administrator, but give yourself credit for being a big hitter.

Learn to accept yourself as a marketer. Accept yourself as creative, resourceful, and clever, one who consistently finds a way, who extends himself in a worthwhile cause. Borrow ideas, from one project for use in another.

The following are affirmations that will be helpful in reforming or growing your self-image.

- I am really excited about this business opportunity.
- I like meeting new people and befriending them.
- It's easy and natural for me to talk with and get to know new people.
- I'm very proud to be in selling.
- I am a creative and resourceful marketer of my services.
- I consistently earn $ _____ per year.
- I produce $ _____ sales volume annually.
- I create a sense of equality with buyers.
- Closing is a very natural, mutual conclusion for me.
- I like marketing our services because I deliver the best message.
- I'm really proud to have the ACME account.

- Each month I generate $ _____ volume in services.
- It's really gratifying to have my article in _____ magazine.
- I have a friendly, warm, and close relationship with _____ .
- I am surrounding _____ with referrals and position inputs about our firm.
- We're breaking into the _____(new)_____ market.
- This is a $10 million dollar company!
- I am making a friend of _____ .
- I think about marketing daily and act on it.

A critical factor is to construct and say these affirmations to yourself in the present tense, as though they had already been achieved. This is the significant difference between affirmations and goals. This is placing the goals in an accomplished state to (1) clarify the more desirable image, and (2) to generate emotional impact, which moves us more than intellectualization. Another important factor here is that while this is a conscious input into the mind, the subconscious accepts information at face value, impartially and without judgment. It accepts information and responds to it. Thus, the present tense enjoyment, excitement, or comfort is vital.

In order for the affirmations to be effective they must be three dimensional: self talked, visualized, and felt. The words alone are mere triggering devices. The imagery, picturing, and visualizing is even more important. You need to see the people, the numbers, the agreements, the settings, and everything. This is a mind manufacturing process which requires imagination and vividness and color, and action.

Further, the accompanying feeling of elation, satisfaction, progress, and most of all, comfort, needs to be generated in your mind. Fortunately, all this gets accepted by your subconscious and thus we improve our self-images.

Unfortunately, the entire process works in the negative just as effectively. Tell yourself you are a klutz who is out of place in selling, picture getting thrown out on your ear, and feeling rejected—see how well that works after a few months! I urge you now before you go on to the next chapter or page to select or construct some positive affirmations like the ones I have listed. Six or seven will do. Plan to use them regularly. Say them to yourself, visualize them successfully, and get enthused and comfortable with them. This may be the most valuable technique you will derive from this book.

AFFIRMATION SHEET

1. GOAL: _____

2. Select one positive adjective you'd like to use in describing you as relates to this goal:

   _____

3. Affirmation: Positive, present tense, as though already achieved, incorporating the adjective:

   _____

   _____

1. GOAL: _____

2. Select one positive adjective you'd like to use in describing you as relates to this goal:

   _____

3. Affirmation: Positive, present tense, as though already achieved, incorporating the adjective:

   _____

   _____

1. GOAL: _____

2. Select one positive adjective you'd like to use in describing you as relates to this goal:

   _____

3. Affirmation: Positive, present tense, as though already achieved, incorporating the adjective:

   _____

   _____

1. GOAL: _____

2. Select one positive adjective you'd like to use in describing you as relates to this goal:

   _____

3. Affirmation: Positive, present tense, as though already achieved, incorporating the adjective:

   _____

   _____

1. GOAL: ————————————————————————

2. Select one positive adjective you'd like to use in describing you as relates to this goal:

————————————————————————————————

3. Affirmation: Positive, present tense, as though already achieved, incorporating the adjective:

————————————————————————————————

————————————————————————————————

1. GOAL: ————————————————————————

2. Select one positive adjective you'd like to use in describing you as relates to this goal:

————————————————————————————————

3. Affirmation: Positive, present tense, as though already achieved, incorporating the adjective:

————————————————————————————————

————————————————————————————————

Now get a small card and copy these affirmations (only) on it and carry the card with you in your wallet. Find two minutes each day to focus on them and feel good about them.

How To Use Affirmations

Now that you have your affirmations, you need to put them to work for you. Here are some suggestions.

1. *Keep them to yourself.* They are selected by you, about you, and are to be used by you. We can dissipate our energy, drive, and creativity when we start blowing off steam generated in our minds. Don't run around talking about what great deeds you are going to accomplish! It's worth remembering that there are a lot of poeple who are perfectly ready, willing, and able to tell you you'll never make it. Why tell such people? Let them throw water on others. What makes them so knowledgeable about your talents, skills and abilities?

2. *Self-talk, picture, and feel these from inside you to the outside.* Be in the meeting, not watching it. Be reading your published article in the magazine. Be making the speech from the podium, not in the audience watching yourself up there.

3. *The time to affirm is any time you are relaxed.* When you are relaxed, your subconscious is more accessible. A relaxed, uncluttered mind is more receptive to new input. The three stages of affirmation require perhaps ten to fifteen seconds for each affirmation. The practice of affirmation can be viewed as an investment in time—probably no more than one to two minutes for all your affirmations. This investment is perhaps the most important one you can make because your thoughts can so significantly direct your behavior and circumstances.

4. *It is not necessary to believe your affirmations.* Belief is a matter of blind faith, and you are not being asked to believe your affirmations. However, you need to *experience* and *feel* them to the point that you become psychologically comfortable with them. When you are comfortable with your affirmations, your behavior will naturally move in their direction.

5. *Learn to let your subconscious perform its function.* The more you practice and become familiar with an affirmation, the more the affirmation will be relegated from the conscious to the subconscious. Once an affirmation is in your subconscious, it is most influential because the behavior you are affirming will become automatic. Automatic behavior is, of course, the ideal. The best way to get an affirmation into the subconscious is constant repetition with words, vivid, successful images, and feelings of pleasure and excitement.

6. *Results will come.* One cannot pinpoint exactly when you will see the results of your affirmations because there is too much variation in affirmations and individuals. However, results *will* come because, once again, you consistently behave in harmony with your self-image.

COMMITMENT

Commitment is a primary source of strength. If you have enough of it, you may very well make up for a lack of knowledge and a poor self-image. Sometimes we are not able to obtain enough answers, techniques, and skills. Sometimes our image of ourselves is not as strong or clear or powerful as we would like it to be. That's when an extra dose of commitment helps see us through.

Supposing you were standing on the side of a body of water and you could not see more than 30-40 feet, but you were compelled to forge on and to keep moving. Suppose further you didn't know the depth of the water or the height of the rocks beneath the surface. You cannot read the current and do not know the size of the sea life that may exist in these waters, but still you want to continue on. Clearly it is difficult under such circumstances to know what to do. Sometimes the right thing to do is to jump in and start swimming because when you do, you make things happen. You have been given many ideas in this book—both from a techniques point of view and an attitude perspective. Perhaps you are not fully armed, fully prepared with all the knowledge you need, or the attitudes you'd like to have—yet there is still the need to go on. Jump in. Make it happen. You have enough tools on how to sell—what counts now is your commitment.

There are several times in life when major forks in the road are presented to us. I'm not referring to the multitude of daily decisions, but those concerning careers, marriage, changes of career paths, sometimes even life and death decisions. Perhaps we are faced with these ten to twelve times in our lives. Once the decision is made, what counts most is the commitment.

You may be facing that sort of decision and commitment now. You may be deciding you're going to be a big hitter, or maybe you've concluded you must sell and market yourself, your ideas, and your services in order to succeed in your discipline. I'd agree if you've come to that conclusion.

I'm sure by now you can see I respect selling and marketing greatly. I don't like or use pitch or spiel. That makes me think of a carnival barker. It's demeaning. I like presentation, explanation, offering, persuasion, leadership. That makes me think of several corporate presidents I know. It brings to mind several religious leaders who are outstanding spokesmen for their ideologies. It reminds me of some political leaders who have excelled in selling and marketing themselves, their ideas, and their services. It even reminds me of a few truly outstanding teachers I know. So part of the purpose of this book has been to sell marketing and selling.

In these last pages I'd like to offer you an experience of mine that highlights several key points of this book. Only a few years ago

I was the president of a firm in the self-improvement field. I had been with that firm for twelve of it's first thirteen years. I sold, managed, taught, created, and eventually ran that business. I could have stayed for as long as I wanted. But I decided to leave. The principals of that firm said that any business I developed for that firm belonged to that firm, and I should not go after their clientele. Because I was going into a business that would likely be competitive with that firm and I didn't want to create legal waves—I agreed. So, at early middle age, I started my own business.

I had no clients, no income, didn't have a lot of reserves nor a lot of time to produce income. I had two houses, three cars, four children to educate, and all the other obligations you are familiar with. I also had the three things necessary to succeed. I knew what it took to start a seminar business. I had helped the other firm get started. I had the knowledge. Secondly, I had a good self-image. I had a clear fix on what kind of lifestyle personally and professionally I wanted for myself and my family. Thirdly, I was committed. I didn't just put my foot in the water. I jumped in. I walked away from the other business and started my own with a full effort. It was the best move I ever made professionally. I've enjoyed it all—the teaching, the creativity, the writing and, yes, the selling and marketing. It's a fun game that I hope you enjoy too and that you get as much enjoyment and reward from those activities as I have.

Here's a selection from W. H. Murray that means a lot to me. Read this while wearing your "marketing and selling hat."

Commitment

Until one is committed, there is hesitancy, the chance to draw back, always ineffectiveness, concerning all acts of initiative and creation there is one elementary truth, the ignorance of which kills countless ideas and splendid plans: that the moment one definitely commits oneself, then providence moves too.

All sorts of things occur to help one that would never otherwise have occurred. A whole stream of events issues from the decision, raising in one's favor all manner of unforeseen incidents and meetings and material assistance, which no man could have dreamt would have come his way.

I have learned a deep respect for one of Goethe's couplets:

"Whatever you can do, or dream you can do, begin it. Boldness has genius, power, and magic in it."

W.H. MURRAY

It has been said that 3 percent of the people in the world make things happen, 10 percent know what is happening, and about 87 percent really don't know what's going on. I won't vouch for the numbers but that's close enough to be real. Another saying goes, "Nothing happens until someone sells something." That's also true. Combining these two statements automatically puts the sellers and marketers in that special 3 percent bracket who make things happen. That in turn makes them more valuable to their firms, colleagues, clients, and customers.

APPENDICES

Appendix A:
Interviews

This appendix consists of an interview conducted by Jerry Derloshon with two professional businesspeople. Both know and relate to the material contained in this book. Their responses to a number of questions are provided to indicate how certain principles on marketing and selling are being applied successfully. Read the interviews and consider how you'd respond to each question. You may even write out your own responses to these questions to get a feel for how you're approaching each content area.

GARY L. DAVIDSON, FOUNDER, WORLD FOOTBALL LEAGUE

Gary L. Davidson, an attorney, has had his offices in Orange County, California, since 1962. He received his Bachelor of Arts Degree from the University of California at Los Angeles in 1958, and also his Doctorate of Jurisprudence from UCLA in 1961. He specialized in corporate and taxation law with emphasis on the real estate industry. His main field of activity during the last ten years has been in finance, again with the emphasis on the real estate industry.

In addition to the practice of law, Davidson has been involved in numerous other business activities. He has been active as a principle in developing and financing numerous real estate projects, ranging from shopping centers to retirement facilities.

Davidson organized the California Real Estate Trust, which has over 3,000 shareholders and is traded over-the-counter. He is the president of the trust. He was part of the group that formed California Properties Pension Fund, an equity real estate corporation. The fund is currently involved in a $50,000,000 offering to corporate retirement trusts. He is a partner in California Financial Group, which is active in the development and financing of commercial real estate projects.

Probably the most well-known of Gary's business endeavors was his founding of the World Football League (WFL). An entrepreneur, Gary Davidson is a professional who markets and sells every day of his working life.

Q: *Some people have a problem seeing themselves as salespersons, and Mike is trying to say to a widespread audience that you need to perceive yourself as a marketer and seller of your services and your ideas. Any thoughts?*

A: I've always thought that I was a sales-oriented person in the sense that I had to sell myself as a lawyer in order to acquire clients. You do that by your personality first, and then after you've practiced law for a while, or any profession, if you have capabilities, you don't need to "sell" any more to a certain extent. Because then the client/buyer comes to you. If you are the greatest heart surgeon, buyers don't care what your personality is, they will just come to you for the services you are going to render. It's the same thing with certain types of product. If you have the very best (say a Porche dealer) you can be a jerk and still sell.

Q: *What you are saying leads to one of the areas that Mike says is a first phase of marketing. He's divided marketing up into four phases. The first phase is creating a public image in terms of who knows you and how well they know you. One of the things he talks about is the importance of articles, speeches, seminars, and brochures. Have you used any of these vehicles?*

A: I personally have not gained any business that I'm aware of from seminars or being a public figure. When I became visible as a public figure I wasn't marketing a service, I was organizing and selling a product franchise (World Football League). That franchise was sold from the publicity about the venture and not necessarily from the publicity about me. People who buy football or hockey franchises buy them because they want to be in the business. In selling real estate syndicates our company goes out and tries to find somebody who has money—which means qualifying the potential buyer. You qualify by being a member of a church, or a rotary group, or a financial group where you can find out who has money. Then you find out if they are interested in real estate or you try to get them interested in something. Most of my contacts in raising money have come from contacts I've made as a lawyer.

Q: *You used your professional activity in establishing a name of quality. Once a public image is going and developing with a number of people, Mike describes a second phase called developing relationships, where you create buyer interest. How do you try to create buyer interest?*

A: That's opening up the market to exposure as compared to a seminar or mailer, and lawyers tend to become known within the community from activities within the community—boards of education, hospital groups, church groups, boys clubs, and so on, just like insurance salesmen or anyone else who needs a client base. That's the initial activity for young attorneys. Initially you give your money to a stockbroker because you like the way he presents his position. Now once he loses your money you stop giving it to him. Once he makes money for you—that establishes his professional credibility. As a lawyer you have one type of sales capability. As a promoter of a product, you may go at it differently. If I'm trying to sell somebody on a franchise (a sports franchise or a real estate syndicate) I'm not necessarily trying to maintain my role as a dignified member of the bar—I'm trying to get the guy to write a check. So my attitude might be a little different.

Q: *Mike talks about a transfer rule—if you are helping a hospital guild, church function, and so on, people may perceive you as conversational, an intelligent worker in that capacity, they might very well transfer your ability to sell a franchise or act as legal representation. Have you seen the transfer rule apply to you personally or to your firm?*

A: I've been involved in situations like a tennis match where people knew I was an attorney have asked me questions informally, and because of the way I've responded, they have subsequently come to me formally as an attorney, which transferred me from just being a tennis partner. That's quite common. If a guy has a problem on his mind and you happen to be an attorney, he's going to ask you about it. That's being available and having exposure. You can also be overly aggressive and that can obviously hurt you. When you are selling a product and the guy knows you are selling the IBM Copier, you do the best you can to sell that copier. As a lawyer, you may be looking not to handle a particular case, but maybe to handle a subsequent case.

Q: *When Mike moves out of the public image role toward developing relationships he enters the selling phase, a track to run on. Are you familiar with the emphasis he places on asking questions?*

A: I read an article Mike did for an airline magazine right after I got through losing a sale in which I had not conducted a good interview. Rather than the interview, I had an opening and went right to the close! As a lawyer, I immediately interview the other person, but as a salesman in that instance, I did not do the interview. It was real dramatic. It was the difference between getting the guy to invest $10,000 and $50,000 and it was, say, a ten minute difference in the presentation. If I would have read that article on asking questions the night before, I would have probably had the dollars. I did not have a rapport with him. As a lawyer, when I talk to people I very seldom do not have a good rapport with them. Through the interview, I establish the credibility. If you are a good attorney you anticipate a lot of the answers to the questions so you are ahead of them a little bit.

Q: *How do you know when the interview is complete?*

A: The key is when you stop talking. A lawyer stops talking when he's got all the facts, and can give them a conclusion or say he needs more time with research.

Q: *The interviewer has to discipline himself just to listen and not talk.*

A: Right.

Q: *Retaining clients—How do you keep the ones you have?*

A: I think that retaining clients in any phase requires communication. The primary thing is communication and second is the quality of the relationship. If a corporation is investing with you and you keep making dividends, that quality is going to stay around. If it's a client and you do a good job for him, they'll stay around.

Q: *How do you keep in touch with clients/customers?*

A: I have never used Christmas cards or that sort of thing. I call people with whom I work a lot. I also believe in personal letters. I believe in *arranging situations* where if I know someone has a particular need for a particular type of equipment, and I know another who has it, I get them together. A lot of attorneys and professional people use cards. I'm not so sure it works. It depends on how large or what type of deal. You have a limitation on how many people you can really be in contact with. So you have to eliminate the weaker and add to the stronger all the time. Because otherwise you shortcircuit your strong clients.

Q: *Goal-setting and action-planning—do you actively support a formal program of goal-setting and action-planning?*

A: I think as a lawyer, goals are often set for you. In other words, you have to get through law school, and you have to pass the bar. Then you get a job or you start your own practice. I don't think professional people have the same tendency to set goals. In sales or sales management you definitely say, "Okay, you have to sell thirty-four units during August or you won't meet your quota." As a lawyer, it's hard to say I'm going to get ten new cases. A lot of times your goals are more general: I'm going to make $100,000 this year. Lawyers are at the mercy a lot of times of people coming to them. I think if you are selling a product or a service, other than a professional service where buyers have to come to you, you can be more goal-oriented with a chance of success. A doctor doesn't come to you and say do you feel sick and let me give you an examination. A lawyer most often has to wait until you have a problem.

Q: *Is there such a character as a professional salesman? Are there certain qualities that one seems to have that you respond to? What qualities go into the guy that's going to come to you and sell you?*

A: On a professional basis I look for the compatibility of the personality, and then the quality of the work product. I have attorneys who work for me that I like both on a personal and a professional basis, but I use them only in areas in which I feel they are strong. Before, when I didn't know as much about law as I do now, I might use the one I like best all the time. I'm trying to take this approach with accounting and other professional services. We have an accountant who isn't a personal friend, but because he knows the accounts and the business, we use him for the longevity factor.

Q: *How important are some behavioral qualities, like good listener, sympathizer, empathizer?*

A: I don't actually look for any of those things, although it probably has an effect on whether I like the guy or not. How do you determine whether you like somebody or how do they determine whether they like you? It involves certain traits that you aren't even aware of. When I'm looking at a guy who is selling me a product, I think I'm fairly easy if I want the product. If I don't want the product, I'm very hard. It is hard for him to talk me into something I don't want. I don't think anyone has ever sold us something we didn't want. I think we've made some bad decisions—we just analyzed things wrong.

GARY CAMPBELL,
PRESIDENT, HOMES FOR SALE MAGAZINE

Gary Campbell is a well-known figure in the home building industry. He is president of *Homes for Sale Magazine,* a major advertising medium for new single and multiple-family dwellings. Campbell has held numerous key positions within the industry, including president of the San Diego California Sales and Marketing Council of the national Building Industry Association (BIA); chairman of the SAM Awards; and a member of the board of directors of the Sales and Marketing Council for eight years.

A versatile individual, Campbell is also a radio broadcaster, covering auto racing action for ABC's Wide World of Sports. Campbell also raced in and won the World Drag Boat Championship. Campbell is a former professional athelete, having played both semi-pro baseball and basketball.

Campbell received his B.A. in marketing and advertising from Woodbury University. He was elected to three four-year terms on the El Monte Union High School District Board of Education, twice holding the position of president of the district representing eleven cities.

Q: *In his introduction to marketing for the professional, Mike covered how important it is for professionals—architects, account- ants, engineers, stockbrokers, and so on—and service organizations such as yours, to see themselves as sellers and marketers. What are your thoughts on the role of the professional in this capacity?*

A: There are two phases to that. You need to see yourself as marketing yourself as well as marketing your service or product. In many ways, the more valuable of the two, as it affects my company, and as Mike was able to relate to my people, is the marketing of ourselves. That really has to happen before anything else. You don't really get through to somebody about your message, about your product or service, until you market yourself. I don't think people think about that when they are in the process of marketing or selling, they just sort of go about it mechanically. Most of us who have grown up in the marketing of a product or service have just sort of subconsciously, without a great deal of thought, discarded the things that didn't work and kept the things that did work without ever looking in the mirror to see what we were all about. One of the things Mike's program does is make you look in the mirror, and then gives you a road to follow in terms of changing what you see in that mirror to what you want to see.

Q: *By marketing yourself are you referring to personal style?*

A: I feel you really need to think about how you are going to develop a really close relationship with the person that you are trying to market or sell to. It takes more than just walking in and sitting down in front of someone's desk and telling him how great you or your product is. You must really develop a relationship with that person so that that person has a belief in you as a *person* and a *professional* in what you have to say or advice you might give as part of your presentation. And certainly the recommendations because the recommendations are what he's going to buy if he buys anything.

Q: *Developing relationships, which you referred to a moment ago, is a second phase Mike talks about. To successfully do that with a number of people, you've got to create a public image. In looking at Mike's telescope depicting the four phases, he lists civic, social, and political activities: brochures, articles, mailings, speeches, school, church and charity activities, as ways to help create what he calls a "public image." Mike says the transfer rule often applies to these* *activities. If you're perceived as warm, energetic, competent, and a hard worker in one enterprise, that attitude often carries over into your profession. How has the issue of a "public image" affected you and your business?*

A: I am a firm believer that the *business professional* is on stage all the time in his professional life. When you go home you take off your makeup and costume and become a father, husband—whatever else you are. When you are in your role as a business professional you are on stage. And all of these things that you do—walk, dress, talk—are very important as are the things you do in your business community. Whether it be civic, social, or whatever. I personally am tremendously involved in association activities because I'm involved in an industry that is relatively close-knit. Within that industry there are several organizations that are very visible and I have made myself a very major part of several of those organizations because of the visibility, and it has been tremendously beneficial. Visibility—to do things that others see so that they begin to gain respect and knowledge of me as a business professional.

Q: *Could you refer to the recent Palm Springs outing you attended as a part of creating a public image?*

A: Absolutely. It was the Southern California Building Industry's annual convention. I accepted the role of chairman of the educational program as part of that event, for visibility. Plus the fact that I happen to feel that it was very needed. It has been basically a fun-and-games type of convention and I think a lot of people this year in this industry are not interested in fun and games. They have had plenty of time in the last couple of months to play fun and games because they haven't been able to do much work. Right now, they are interested in what is going to help them get back on the track. It proved to be correct because we probably had about seven or eight times the usual number of attendees.

Another example of what I do to create a public image: I was elected Monday evening as president of the Sales and Marketing Council of the Building Industry Association. This is something that is going to take a tremendous amount of my time. Going through the chairs to get to this point has taken a tremendous amount of my time. I do it for two reasons. The most selfish and the most important is that it gives me a tremendous amount of visibility and credibility among the other professionals in my field. The thing is,

I happen to believe that the Sales and Marketing Council and the people that make up that council are a very important and viable group of people. They can accomplish a tremendous amount to help this industry and I feel that they need guidance, push, and motivation to get things accomplished. I feel I am that type of person. I motivate people and get things accomplished by providing leadership and direction. That's why I accepted the role. The amount of time should be devoted to running this business but not only indirectly but directly it will benefit this company for years to come, because of the contacts I will make and the visibility that I will get.

Q: *Even outside business are you still on stage?*

A: My personal feeling is we all lead a number of different roles in our life. The role I play as a business professional I feel that I am on stage all the time. When I go home I'm on stage as a husband. When my kids come to visit I'm on stage as a father. I go to the tennis club to play tennis and I'm on stage as Bjorn Borg. (That's who I'd like to be!) You must be ever conscious of your image.

Q: *What you're suggesting is, by creating a public image, the contacts will come. While you may spend a year heading a committee or being involved in an association, in the long run, your efforts will be rewarded—you'll increase the number of contacts. Once you do this, you need, as you suggested earlier, to develop relationships with your contacts. Mike has listed doing your homework, third party support, social engagements, introductions, seeking advice, making referrals, and demonstrating your capabilities. Comment on how you get close with the contacts—how do you develop relationships with the contacts you make?*

A: Homework is the first thing you have to do. Develop and perfect the knowledge of the field you are interested in; social, civic, or in my case it would be the building industry. I have knowledge based on having done my homework that would be impressive to people I interface with. I think that is all-important because no one wants to spend time with someone from whom they feel they aren't getting something. They must feel some gratification from it. You don't want to spend time with the nicest person in the world when they are just a blob when it comes to whatever your conversation is about. Where your interests come together, you need to have a level of communication. If there is nothing there, then there is no similarity of interest or common ground. You have to do your home-work so that you are knowledgeable in your field and can present yourself as being knowledgeable and have information that the people you are talking with desire. So they have to perceive *value* in the relationship with you or you don't have a relationship. I think you have to do your homework to have something of substance. In terms of the other things, I think in the area of third party support and introductions, Mike mentioned it very early on to us and I think everyone in my company uses it very effectively. When we go to a place where a lot of people we want to meet are congregating, we will know a percentage of them, say a third or a half. Those people, many of them, know the others present, and just saying very openly and honestly, "I've never met Herb Schwartz. I'd really like to meet him. I know he's a friend of yours," is an extremely effective way to get introduced and start building relationships. The one thing it does is accomplish an introduction. But by being introduced by this friend of his, you are being endorsed.

Q: *Let's take your story about Mr. Schwartz a step further. You have had through third party support, an introduction to him. How do you actually achieve the goal of developing relationships, that is, to get buyer interest?*

A: Again it comes back to homework. You must have something that he will perceive as a *value* to be interested in a relationship. How much value he sees in it depends on how far the relationship is going to go. Also, it will hinge on what your particular taste in people is and how you react to him. It relates to the importance of being able to read the reactions that people have to the things you do and say. If you walk up to someone and right away you sense negative vibes you know you either have the wrong suit on or you have parted your hair wrong or something.

The same is true if you are watching the reactions during the course of a conversation. If he says, "How are things going?" and I say, "Fine," and I ask him the same question and he says, "Things are going terrible," I say, "Well, the guy down the street is really doing pretty well." You will immediately get a reaction from him. He is either going to be interested or perhaps he already knows that and has built up a resentment. The point is, when you begin to interface, watch closely for the reactions in that person. In terms of the direction the conversation goes and the information that you part, that is how you build a relationship. You have to again go right back to the basics of taking the positives a step further and getting rid of the negatives as you see his reaction to what you are talking about.

Q: *Now that you've learned from Mr. Schwartz that he is generally open or receptive to you and your product/service, that is "buyer interest" actually exists, you need to move toward the selling phase. How do you do this in Mr. Schwartz's case for example?*

A: At almost any meeting I wouldn't start selling this guy unless he is outright trying to draw out information about my publication. Even then, I would almost hold back to the extent that it would be more effective for me at that time to develop a specific appointment and talk to him about how our service can help him at a later time. That would be the perfect situation. For the moment, stick to conversation about the business, what I know about it, and how I have helped other people in similar situations so that he develops interest in wanting more information. That manifests itself in my ability to get an appointment set with him.

Q: *As you enter the selling phase, Mike teaches what variables the professional needs to pay attention to—more homework, where the meeting should take place, office arrangements, supporting documents. What things do you emphasize early in the selling phase, even before you make an actual "presentation"?*

A: What we are talking about is the ideal situation. A lot of times I am hampered by time. Basically, the way I try to do it and urge my people to follow through is to do a significant amount of homework on what the problems and circumstances are of this man's company. What he's interested in as it relates to what I can do for him is selling houses. So what I need to find out is as much information as I can on where his projects are, how many he has, price range, type of product, who the customer they are after is, and basically build up as part of my presentation how my publication is going to answer the problems that he is going to encounter without using my publication. It is a very simple process to determine. I usually talk to the salespeople in the sales office in his company, who are the ones that can give me direct data on all the things I mentioned, including who the buyer is, the type of buyer, in terms of income level and so forth. Then what I have to do is take a vast resource of data we have here and narrow it down to the specific data that is going to specifically apply. I have everything to zero right in on the problem that he already knows he has. All I have to do in terms of selling him on using my publication is convince him that I have the answer to his problem.

Q: *Do you perceive any difference or value in meeting in his office or yours?*

A: I would say it's always his, or on a neutral ground. A lot of times I'll meet someone and say, "How about lunch at noon," because I like to get them out of their office when I can. I'll pick them up and take them to lunch or meet them at a lunch or breakfast place. It's better to get them out of their office environment. The reason for that is the interruption problem. But you have their total attention when you have them away from the office. You also have them for a reasonable length of time where you don't have to worry about taking five minutes of time to get your whole pitch in and build a relationship at the same time. I much prefer to sit down with someone and build a relationship very subtly without their realizing it—get my qualifications and background into the thing so that there is credibility. When I say something, he believes it. When I recommend something he considers it. I think that is very important before we ever get to the selling stage.

Q: *Now that you've done the necessary preparations required in the selling phase, you are ready to present your service, idea, or product. Mike refers to this in steps as a track to run on. He outlines four steps—the opening, the interview, the responding presentation, and the natural conclusion. Let's start with the opening aimed at piquing curiosity, warning, or providing a benefit. What are your thoughts?*

A: An opening is something that needs to be preplanned. The rest of the presentation you pretty much have to come up with as you are going. But the opening really should be preplanned and thought out because you are on a different ground. Say you are in his office. He has a different attitude and feeling about it at that point because he knows you are there to sell him. When you are meeting him in a social situation, his friend was there and he felt a little protection in the situation. Now he realizes he is very vulnerable. He just might buy. So he has a different attitude and approach to you. You must take that into consideration. You have to have something planned out so that it will immediately get the point across that there is a benefit in it for him. And yet for me, it can't be crass commercialism because that's not me. I have to be me. I have to be natural with what I do. The right people can walk in and start twisting someone's arm and they don't feel resentment for it. I don't see myself as that person. I don't operate that way.

I operate in what I consider to be a higher level, and I try to operate with the president of a company, who is the decision maker. He may even have with him the marketing director, who is the actual buyer. But the decision maker is where we are at so I have to be very careful I don't injure someone else's feelings who we already stepped over.

Q: *Do you or any of your people write out openings?*

A: I have done that. It's rare. It's very important to get it started right. If you go into an in-depth kind of an interview having thought out all the steps you are going to go through and what that opening means to the other steps, then you are at least going to have the thing thought out, even if the opening does not go well.

Q: *If you've had a successful opening, you've either piqued curiosity, warned of a danger, or established a benefit. Mike is adamant when he says, that is not the time to pop the closing question. Before you do any such thing, you've got to conduct an effective interview. You've got to get specific needs and wants out on the table. How do you conduct such interviews and what key points would you emphasize?*

A: I like to try to have all the information that I'm going to get out of the interview before I go because you ask better questions. It also makes you much more knowledgeable. When you do your homework you also need to have information about what the competition is doing around him. So that when you are specifically talking to him about what he's doing, while he's doing it, how successful he is, and so forth, you really have something that you can specifically drive home to him in terms of what we find best. Is someone else doing the same thing he is doing, or trying to do the same thing he is doing, who has found us to be tremendously successful? That seems to get through to these people stronger than anything. So that is what we try to do—to set ourselves up so that when he describes himself in the interview we drive home our main selling pitch, how we solved the similar problem down the street.

Q: *Through an effective interview in your case, you're going to determine that the other person needs your service—a lawyer can establish this, a tax accountant, a stockbroker. Through your questions, you don't tell them about you. Rather, they tell you about themselves and what their needs/wants are. An effective interview subsequently should call for a response from you, or as Mike calls it, a* responding presentation. *The interview then, should take up most of the time of the meeting. Is this true for you?*

A: I find I spend 20-25 percent of the interview talking and the rest of it listening. That's what I prefer. I am there to learn and ultimately to sell. Most importantly to learn. Like Mike said, you don't learn anything with your mouth open. If you are asking the right, succinct questions, you are getting a lot back from this guy you can use to drive the point home to him.

Q: *Listening is so important. What do you do to make sure you're really hearing what the other person is saying?*

A: By really concentrating on what the guy is saying, and not letting your mind either wander or race ahead. It is easy to do in that kind of situation, the guy is rattling on, and saying things you already know. But you have to be interested, attentive and more important, concentrate and digest what he is saying. If he says something you don't anticipate, your mind will be off somewhere else and you'll miss it. That can blow your whole situation. Attention to what he is saying is extremely important. What is even more difficult for me in the way of a discipline—and I have found it to be even more important—is that you must read this person as the interview is going on. You have to watch him. You have to feel what is going on and handle the reaction to what he is saying and what he is feeling. I think it was not a natural thing for me to sit down with somebody that I was trying to sell something to and really pay a lot of attention to what was going on in them. I felt like I was on stage and I was there to perform. As I've gotten deeper into Mike's material, I've realized that is not the case at all. I'm not there to perform, I'm there to learn and to interact with this person and ultimately *solve the problem.* First you have to create in his mind that he does have a problem, and then establish the fact that you can solve it. That's what the interview process is suppose to do.

Q: *So a successful interview leads to a responding presentation which fills a need, provides a service, or solves a problem. Mike makes the point that if you open well, interview well, and respond well to what's surfaced in the interview, the close should come easily. He doesn't even use the term close, he refers to reaching a mutual agreement as a* natural conclusion. *He says it'd be unnatural if a satisfactorily mutual conclusion wasn't reached after successfully doing the first three steps. Do you agree with his thinking?*

A: Through my entire career in selling and as a manager of other salespeople, the big stigma with salespeople is *the close.* Mike says, "The close is no big deal!" If you do everything else right, opening, interview, and response, the close is automatic. You don't have anything to do at the close. I think that is such a tremendous concept. I have really pushed it with my people, and it has been the single most effective thing we've learned. It's something that all salespeople can relate to. I've had Mike come to groups of salespeople as a speaker for seminars, and if you watch the reaction of the audience when he drives his point home that if you do all these other things, the close is no big deal—it's like taking weight off their shoulders.

Q: *What are some of Mike's thoughts about retaining clients that are meaningful to you?*

A: My pesonal style is to retain personal relationships, and not just to retain them but to continue improving them. I think it's an obvious thing that you must continue to provide good service. Whatever it takes to get the job done to make his business relationship with you must be done. In addition you have to continue to fulfill your role as a friend, a person the buyer would like to get to know better because you have something to offer—either in the way of advice, information, or just companionship from a conversational standpoint. Or maybe he perceives you to be someone important in the industry that he would like to align himself with. To do this, you must know what the other person's interests are. I have several people that I'll go to lunch with as part of maintaining my relationship and we'll hardly talk business. Ultimately, we'll get around to talking about business and how it's doing.

Q: *Mike talks about a* preventive medicine *approach to retaining clients. Rather like an annual checkup where you and the client or customer set everything aside, and the question is asked, "How am I doing?" It gives the client an opportunity to tell you what strengths* *or weaknesses may exist with you or your service as perceived by them. Do you have any thoughts on the subject?*

A: I'm doing something right now for the first time. I sent out fifty-five letters to clients, and some people whom I would like to have as clients, asking them their opinion of our publication and people. I've done it through a management consultant organization that I'm going to spend three days with next week as part of a learning process. The information will be brought to me at that time. It's the first time I've done anything like that. Anything of that nature has been done on a one-on-one basis. Quite honestly, I've always been taught that the last thing you want to ask is, "How are we doing for you?" The answer may be, "You're not!" But I don't believe that. I feel that what you have to do is establish a very assumptive type of relationship. You just gladly go over the whole thing. I try to separate how the publication is doing as an advertising media and how we as a whole are functioning in our servicing of their account, because I think the two are not necessarily integral.

Q: *How about the point about happy clients and customers acting as a best source for new business—referrals, and so on? Do you find that well-served clients help with new input into your business?*

A: Not only do well-served clients tell the story to others on their own, you can get the story out of them and repeat it yourself. When I find someone who is doing well and saying good things about us, I'm just dragging everything I can get out of him and encouraging him to broadcast that message to everyone else he knows. I love to bring the very satisfied customer into a situation where a potential customer or someone who is very negative happens to be at a meeting or social occasion and get the two of them talking, especially about the publication.

Q: *Another section of the book is devoted to what Mike calls the most important game:* You. *Chapters are devoted to* goal-setting, *the* self-image, thought processes, conditioning, *and other concepts aimed at helping us get out of life exactly what we want—personally and professionally. You're familiar with this area of Mike's teaching. How have these points affected you and your employees?*

A: It has probably affected me more than most people because I happen to be one of those people who was not very conscious of my self-image, or my goals, or anything else prior to the time that I first met Mike. I happen to feel that it is tremendously important. Especially in a sales/service organization. Because we are a sales/service organization it is important for all of us here to be very conscious of our images and all that our images mean to the people we are exposed to. When I am looking for a salesperson, my feeling is they have to think they are king of the world. They must have a tremendous self-image. Self-image in my opinion is difficult to change. For sales professionals, it is an all important element.

In our type of work I've long since made the decision that it was necessary to have our people portray a particular type of image in the field: One of confidence in themselves, in our publication, and in our position in the industry. All of the people that I have brought into this company and have been successful and are with the company today, are people that have felt good about themselves to start with. The rest of it they grow with or it grows with them. They have a true sense of confidence.

Q: *How about the importance and application of goal-setting and action plans. Relate this to you and your business as far as the individual professional is concerned.*

A: I attempt to structure a plan for goal-setting with all of my people. A person needs to have serveral sets of goals: professional, personal, whatever. In some cases they are interrelated. I try to provide an environment for the people to do their goal-setting. Goal-setting and short- and long-term strategic planning is valuable not only for a company but for individuals, too. You really can't get anywhere if you don't know where you're going.

Appendix B:
Questions
and Responses

During numerous years of presenting seminars, workshops, and conducting sales training in-house for client companies, questions often come up that have been expressed by a wide cross-section of professionals. The following is a collection of the twenty most often asked questions about marketing and selling for professionals, and how I respond to those questions.

Q: *When do you bring up money, fee, price, and so on?*

A: You don't. Let the buyer bring it up, or, after he has committed to act, you bring it up. Concentrate on the problem at hand—the need, the want and the solution, and the responses—not on price. Price is irrelevant if you don't answer the person's wants first. Price is too frequently a problem in the seller's mind. The buyer is first interested in resolutions. The seller should be interested first in the resolution and its benefits. The doctor concentrates on the illness or injury, and regaining health. His fee comes later. Ditto for you.

Q: *Will the buyer really tell you that much private information about his firm or situation?*

A: Yes, if you make it easy for him to do so. By building credibility with incisive questions, and by showing genuine interest in his answers you will gradually open him up. Start with easy, general open-ended questions, and listen carefully to what the buyer says. The longer the buyer talks the more likely he is to reveal his real hand. If he believes in your interest (and of course your confidentiality) he'll tell you intimate, vital, valuable data. Further, you have the right to find out if you maintain that confidentiality. You need to know to prescribe properly.

Q: *Do you recommend one-on-one or team selling?*

A: I prefer one-on-one because of the intimacy that can be more easily developed. I believe more cards get placed on the table than with groups. My experience is to get the buyer to so directly relate to me and what I can do for him that he feels the need to bring me into his confidence. Team selling, however, does have the advantage of team members hitchhiking on each others' ideas and bringing up points the others may overlook.

Q: *Who should go on the selling presentation if more than one person participates?*

A: The following three elements should always be present in a selling situation: a quarterback—someone who understands selling and marketing and calls the plays, an expert on the topic at hand, and someone who will be dealing directly with the client on a day-to-day basis, many times on the client's premises. Sometimes these three essential elements exist in one person, sometimes two or three. But remember, you are not there in a selling situation to solve problems, conduct services, or save the buyer. Instead you are there to get a commitment to do one or more of these things. So the prominent hat to be worn is that of selling even though you may want the buyer to perceive you as consultant, expert, professional, or something else. In a selling mode your goal remains that of getting favorable action or commitment. The selling-oriented person is usually best at this. The expert is important and so is the on-the-job worker. But he will not get the job as often as a professional who has an acceptable level of basic knowledge of the subject at hand, and a superior understanding of the selling process.

Q: *How do you get known?*

A: I make speeches, write letters, make phone calls, design and send brochures, create good contacts who will generate referrals, train contacts to refer, send mailer reminders of my subject material, and lastly, I attempt to do good work. Writing articles and using them after they are published by mailing them to prospective buyers, and listing the programs and speeches I give on a piece of corporate stationery all help my reputation.

Q: *How much time should you spend building rapport at the beginning of a sales presentation?*

A: Very little—two to five minutes. The best rapport can be built later in the give-and-take of the presentation, and after the meeting. The buyer is busy and you should respect your own time because it's important too. If the meeting, however, is aimed at getting to know each other, then perhaps the whole meeting may be devoted to rapport-building. Know the nature of the meeting to determine the amount of rapport building you should do.

Q: *How can I get speeches?*

A: Start by giving them for nothing. All clubs, service organizations, schools, and church meetings are looking for speakers—especially at those prices! Graduate yourself to $50, then to $100, and up. Call a low fee an honorarium. People will wonder what you "usually get" (something higher). Practice at school PTA meetings and company meetings, make toasts, and so on. The best speech-making technique is not making a speech but being yourself and conversing with the audience. I use an outline—key words that trigger a whole series of thoughts on a single topic. The topics must be in a good sequence that flows. I prefer a thought-provoking beginning, a fully developed and involving middle, and an uplifting ending. Short, fast, upbeat speeches are better than long, detailed, slow speeches. Another technique I use is to invite a question and answer period after a short, fast "highlight" talk (which I hope provokes questions). This is then followed by an inspirational ending. I usually use a reading that has inspired me, or that I can introduce by tying it into part of the speech. I recommend Toastmasters, and public speaking courses, but I especially recommend experience. Being natural and one's self and talking about what we know well is also of primary importance. Do your homework! Nothing substitutes for knowing the topic.

Q: *Do you have a formal contract?*

A: Yes, which I send in the mail immediately after a verbal agreement is reached. A handshake or a telephone agreement is followed by a short, simple, clear, one-page contract that states pertinent facts, and buyer and seller obligations. Included in this is a substantial downpayment with a cancellation clause. This says we are serious. Dates are of great importance because selling ourselves, our ideas, or services, is usually tied to that dimension. All travel and hotel expenses are included. The contract should never take a long time to arrive on the buyer's desk. It is a quick response that states, "Here's how we play the game."

Q: *What about after you've done a program for someone, do you do anything else?*

A: I always send a thank you. I write it myself and send it on personal stationery. These notes go to the president and the person who asked me to conduct the session. A recording of these notes is inserted in the company's folder in our files. A 3 × 5 card file is made for three groups of people: Green for individual clients who attend my seminars, pink for companies who bring me in to do a program, and white for prospective attendees or buyers of my services. These files are carefully culled and screened once a year to keep them current.

Q: *Suppse your diagnostic findings indicate a want or a need that you can't fill? What do you do?*

A: Walk away from it, or continue the interview until you've found another legitimate place where you can help. Walking away shows a sense of integrity and it builds credibility for a second chance. If you can't provide the necessary aid you might consider getting someone else to help. Finding another resource specialist is still a way of helping and building credibility.

Q: *What happens if the buyer wants to buy something he doesn't really need?*

A: If he doesn't need it, tell him so. If he could use it, however, and it is legitimate, sell it to him for two reasons. First, you now have an opportunity to display outstanding service—give him the best you've got and educate him to what he may truly need later. Second, you are now holding off competition. The buyer will not likely utilize the services of others in your field of expertise while you are working for him and giving him outstanding service.

Q: *What is your fee structure?*

A: I have a standard daily fee, half-day fee, and speech fee. I vary it depending on the location and convenience or inconvenience for me. If the occasion is more than a year into the future I'll charge a higher than standard fee because if I'm going to commit my time that far in advance I am building the rest of my schedule around that event and I'd better make it worth it. If the location is far away or difficult to get to I'll charge a higher-than-standard fee also—for the same reason. The reverse is also occasionally true. If the assignment is near, convenient or fits nicely into my schedule than I may charge less than standard fees.

Q: *What are some of your sales and marketing aids or tools?*

A: My program information sheet has proven to be well-received by prospective clients and buyers alike. People seem grateful to have a short, clear list of services they can refer to. We can then talk about these itemized services on the phone with lists in front of both of us. Any article I've written or had written about me is reproduced on good-looking paper and included in any mailing that is concerned about the topic of the article. The article indicates I'm an "expert!" A good brochure is a necessity for image promotion. At least one picture is essential.

Outlines of program content or complete texts (perhaps what is actually used in seminars) are sometimes the useful tool that will impress the buyer. Sometimes people want to check referrals. Encourage this. Provide them with evidence, names, titles, company names, addresses, and phone numbers. These should be people who are (1) high level, (2) friends (not foes), (3) agreeable to such inquiries. Use primarily financial references for financial inquiries, aerospace references for aerospace inquiries, and so on. Sometimes people like to see the product. I'll invite them to meetings or conferences or seminars I'm conducting—with the approval of the paying client.

Q: *How much do you rely on referrals, that is getting individuals to help you generate business?*

A: A great deal. I believe that if I pick the right clients they are happy and even flattered to help. The right clients are high level, more than satisfied, and possess an appreciation of sales and marketing. Usually at some point in our relationship I feel them out to see what their feelings are about such things. If it is positive I mention that at some future, unknown time I may refer someone to them. Without exception they have been receptive. And without exception when they have been contacted by potential buyers they have been helpful—sometimes the pivotal input on the sale. I frequently write notes to them and thank them for their help.

When the referring source is in a large company and helping me to continue to promote my services within that company I am most appreciative and show it. I'll buy them lunch, send them a book, even offer to have a close relative attend one of my seminars as my guest to show that appreciation for their help.

Q: *What percentage of your time is devoted to M & S (marketing and selling) and what percentage is devoted to your discipline (teaching, preparing, reading, and so on)?*

A: I'll estimate this to be 50-50. This may seem high to professionals, but in my case it's necessary. People do not eat, wear or live in what I provide, nor is it legislated as a need, nor do my services put off death, taxes, or war. Further, people can procure services like mine elsewhere readily. Therefore, it is clearly to my benefit to create a publicly perceived service that is unique, better or that provides a hope of betterment. I'll never forget the time I arranged a meeting between a very young, naive priest, who was principal of a catholic high school and wanted to expand it and the most successful school fundraiser I knew. The priest asked the fundraiser what amount of his time he spent on fundraising (marketing in this case). "About 85 percent" was the answer and the young cleric (and I) were a bit overwhelmed at that. The source was a mature, academically accredited principal who had started and seasoned the finest private school in the county. He was asked regularly to advise others in school fundraising and was frequently offered principal (headmaster) positions at other fine schools.

In education, seminar-giving, law, architecture, consulting, and so on, it is the same: The greater number of people who know you favorably, the greater your potential for profits. The business of getting known favorably is a major task and requires a major time commitment.

Q: *How long does it take to get the business up to satisfactory levels?*

A: It varies with the perception of you in your marketplace. The greater number of the "right" people (decision makers, buyers, and so on) who know you favorably when you start, the easier and faster you'll attain the success level. An important factor to remember is that the telescope needs to be fed at the beginning, middle, and end of your career as long as you want to continue in it. The telescope can and will dry up if you fail to continue to put things into it. This happened to me early in my career, and I learned my lesson to constantly market.

Q: *What do you think of freebies?*

A: Not much. I try to avoid them. However, I frequently offer a business ally an extra-something that is added to the service I agreed to provide. The extra is typically more services, like a seminar for someone as my guest, a youth conference attendance as my guest, a speech for an honorarium (tiny fee), a training session for facilitators using one of my video tape series, and so on. If people don't pay for something they don't give it enough value or use it well, or appreciate it. Sometimes someone may offer an assignment and use good exposure as the only pay. If you need it okay—for an honorarium. A professional can offer his services wisely as a means to thank, barter, or encourage additional business. He is probably missing some opportunities if he doesn't ask, "What, among all the services I provide, can I use to further my efforts with this potential client/buyer?"

Q: *At what level in a company do you start in your effort to sell a company on buying your service?*

A: The higher the better. If you can influence the president to use your service personally, do it. If you can influence the president to support or endorse the use of your services, do it. If not the president, get to a senior or executive vice president. It is consistently easier to "sell down" than "sell up." Use good taste and sell each person on each echelon thoroughly. Be careful not to assume anything, with any of the "next lower levels" just because you have the president's blessing. Each person wants and deserves to believe in your service.

Sometimes your only entre is at a lower level. This is not usually good, but if it is your only shot make it. Plant the seeds for moving up in the organization, but in order to reach more and more people you must reach the more influential people in the organization. They control more money.

Personnel managers are usually helpful to facilitate mid-level training. They are not usually helpful in executive-level development. When an executive is sold on you and what you offer, cultivate that relationship so he will help sponsor you. Meet with him, seek his counsel, make recommendations on what you want to happen (based, of course, on your experience) give him credit, make him a hero for finding you.

Q: *How do I get the time to do this marketing and selling activity?*

A: You make it by structuring your priorities, and turning on your antenna when you are doing some of the social, community, leisure, recreational, or church activities in which you're already engaged. Make selling and marketing a higher priority and delegate or procrastinate on some of the other activities. Catch up later. Increased gross sales volume properly priced will provide you with the means to cultivate and enhance your discipline. Seeing all situations as a means of contacts, and ultimately business, will help you turn on your antenna more readily.

Q: *What differences do you see between a professional salesperson versus a professional person who recognizes the need for selling?*

A: The salesperson is primarily interested in moving a product or service. His or her activity is narrow, clear, and managed by others. The professional who sells is primarily concerned with his or her professional discipline—architecture, law, accounting, counsulting, and so on. However, this individual, in order to be both a whole professional and an effective one, needs to let people know of his or her abilities and persuade others to use his or her services. Selling and marketing is a part of the profession, not the whole. Most professionals tend to manage themselves. It is important to recognize the difference between a professional and a salesperson—for selling and marketing purposes. The professional wants the buyer to perceive him or her as a professional, not as a salesperson. This enables the professional to maintain two things: his or her expertise and his or her dignity.

Appendix C:
Articles

I have used articles either written by me and contributed to magazines or ones written about me to accomplish either of two or both of the following objectives. First, to create a public image or second, to reinforce my credibility and help me develop relationships.

HUMAN POTENTIAL MOVEMENT

By Jerry Derloshon

Mike McCaffrey wasn't happy living in Los Angeles, and working in the guest relations department at NBC. So he quit. He moved his family to Newport Beach and then thought about what he might do for a living. At 28, his bachelors degree in business administration from UCLA and the letters "NBC" on his resume didn't bring in a raft of job offers. He was searching for something. He didn't know exactly what it was, but he knew he'd recognize it when he found it.

At the recommendation of a friend, McCaffrey attended an Executive Dynamics Seminar on

Reprinted from the April, 1978 issue of *The Executive* of Orange County. Reprinted by permission of Executive Publications, Inc., Newport Beach, Ca.

personal development and company effectiveness. Afterwards, he knew he wanted to go into the seminar-giving business, to teach and instruct people in a subject that he found fascinating—self-image psychology. His early entry into the business education field made him a forerunner in the human potential movement.

Within a year he joined the P.A.C.E. organization which stands for "personal and company effectiveness." P.A.C.E. was a leading national business seminar firm headed by James Newman, an Executive Dynamics dropout. McCaffrey moved up the ranks with zeal, became president, and stayed with the company for 12 years. Then he felt it was time to make another change. He cut the umbilical cord and went out on his own.

With a new mortgage on a house in Laguna's secluded Emerald Bay and the addition of a fourth child to his family, McCaffrey knew he couldn't endure the slow process of building a company. After bouncing alternatives back and forth, he talked a Hollywood agent into watching his presentation with the idea of developing self-image psychology into a television show.

Two independent local television stations picked up the show, which he called "Formulas For High Achievement." McCaffrey funded the first two months from his own pocket; a sponsor picked up the tab for another six months; and after that, the station had accumulated such favorable response, it paid for an additional three months of programming.

McCaffrey lured a number of prominent persons on the show as his guests; among them Werner Erhard, founder of EST; astronaut James Lovell; Tim Gallwey, author of the Inner Game of Tennis; Sugar Ray Robinson; and nationally known business figures William Oncken and Mike Vance. His format was to introduce them to the audience and discuss achievement with them and how they attained it. The host was picking up as many tips as the audience, to be sure, and in the meantime, getting great exposure for it.

When he wasn't in the studio, he was on the phone drumming up business, or making presentations. Within the last four years he has success-fully established himself as one of the dominant national figures in the personal development scene. His clients include the New York-based accounting firm of Touche Ross & Co., E. F. Hutton, General Dynamics, Young Presidents' Organization (YPO), Mission Viejo Co. and Continuing Education Corporation.

More than 100,000 people have shared his expertise in the areas of self-image psychology. "I'm not a psychologist," he muses; "I just practice it."

In addition to giving seminars in every major city in the U.S. and several cities in Canada and Mexico, McCaffrey conducts several three-day personal development seminars a year at Coto de Caza, attended mainly by couples. The focus of the seminars is on communications, mutual goal setting and achievement in the framework of the family and the corporation. For that reason he calls his programs FOCUS seminars which is an abbreviation for Freedom of Choice and Understanding Success. And he has his own definition of success—"knowing your values and conducting your personal and professional life around them."

Riding on the crest of the human potential movement, McCaffrey's content is more appropriate today than ever before. With the growing emphasis on the development of the human resource through such approaches as EST, transactional analysis and behavior management, his focus on self-image psychology—or as he refers to it—"the psychology of wellness," makes him a sought after resource specialist. He addresses groups as intimate as 10-15 and as large as 400. His programs range from 45-minute lectures such as he gave recently at a YPO university, to half-day, full-day and three-day in-depth workshops.

"Everyone has concepts . . . impressions . . . that we form all our lives," says McCaffrey, "that dictates how well we utilize our skills." Referring to a Biblical phrase: "As a man thinketh in his heart, so is he," McCaffrey brings people in touch with their own view of themselves and how this has affected the decisions they've made in their lives.

One of the most popular seminars deals with

the concept of responsibility which McCaffrey defines as "a willingness to accept the consequences of our choices." Not unlike Dr. Wayne Dyer, author of *Your Erroneous Zones*, who suggests we are "the sum total of our choices." McCaffrey's message hit its mark with Phillip J. Reilly, president of the Mission Viejo Co., who after attending a seminar, has been sending employees of the company regularly. The same is true for Ronald L. Rodgers, president of the Bank of Newport. Still another McCaffrey seminar participant is Jack Linkletter, president of the YPO worldwide, and head of his own cattle ranch, meat packing company, and land development firm.

"Many of the people who attend my seminars don't actually need to," says McCaffrey, "But they come anyway, to affirm, to be reinforced." Some participants have attended as many as four of his three-day personal development seminars, and have vowed to attend a fifth.

With offices in Newport Beach, the president of Mike McCaffrey and Associates conducts business with a capable, right-arm secretary named Hortense Bosshard who's been with him since he left P.A.C.E. in 1974.

"She's great. She anticipates, has all the skills, puts together all the seminar packages, manages the finances, does all the coordination," McCaffrey says. "She lets me stay home and play tennis," a favorite pastime, along with spending time with his wife Sharon (O'Malley), their daughters Kathleen and Megan, and sons Mike Jr. and Patrick.

The McCaffrey's live what he calls "an idyllic life" and one they have created "by design," as opposed to many lives that are lived, as he puts it, "by default."

As far as the future is concerned, McCaffrey is thinking about ways to work less—he now works about 40 weeks a year—and makes more. He says the secret is "in first discovering what you like to do and then discovering a way to make money doing it." And with a smile he adds, "I practice everything I preach."

"RESPONSIBILITY" IS THE INTENSE THEME OF McCAFFREY'S THREE-DAY SEMINARS AT COTO DE CAZA'S RELAXED RESORT

THURSDAY EVENING

It's a casual, relaxed atmosphere. People have come to Coto de Caza from all over the country and many are winding down after hours of travel. Many are there with their employers' blessings, with the companies footing the bill for the three-day seminar. Management has seen the positive effects on other participants. Others are paying out-of-pocket because they have heard from people that it could very well be the most valuable weekend of their lives.

Most of the 24 participants have come in pairs. Others are single. The meeting room, nestled in the quiet Saddleback hills, is filled with light conversation. The host is greeting people and matching names to faces. He is poised, articulate and comes across as warm and genuine.

After introductions are made, Mike McCaffrey, seminar-giver, eases naturally into one of his favorite topics—responsibility—which he says is the "key to freedom." He says the choices which each of us have made have determined, for the most part, our circumstances in life. We are responsible—not our parents, not our teachers and not the government. He demonstrates how the human system is self-determining and explains what natural freedom is and how we can have more of it. McCaffrey emphasizes there is a strong correlation between "successful" people and the degree of responsibility they are willing to accept for their decisions good and bad. Participants are at once drawn to his personality. Full of enthusiasm, his presentation is animated

Reprinted from the April, 1978 issue of *The Executive* of Orange County. Reprinted by permission of Executive Publications, Inc., Newport Beach, Ca.

and he moves constantly while he talks. His well-rehearsed format is made lively with original anecdotes which McCaffrey injects humorously and with the timing of a polished comedian.

FRIDAY

The first morning session is devoted to values and the importance of integrating values into daily life. "They are not constant, they change, are strengthened and diminished," says McCaffrey. He offers an insight into the self-image concept and describes how this image affects business and personal relationships. He follows the session with a discussion on conditioning techniques to building what he says is the single most important characteristic in all human systems—self-esteem. McCaffrey tells the group, "Self-esteem is an inner feeling of worth which forms the catalyst for healthy self-fulfillment; it is knowing yourself and liking what you know."

The remainder of the day deals with the concept of image impression and psychological methods for enlisting the subconscious mind to help develop potential. McCaffrey quotes a favorite saying of his, "Dreams make plans come true, it's not the other way around."

SATURDAY

Crystallization of goals and movement toward their achievement is the subject of a morning session. The leader says: "Without goals we're directionless and motionless; we stagnate, or worse yet, grow in a negative direction." Participation exercises help the group evaluate and put into practice the new goals they have set. The afternoon and evening is free. Some play tennis at Vic Braden's tennis college; others walk and talk, and think. That evening, the group meets for dinner and McCaffrey plays some ragtime on the piano.

SUNDAY

The morning session covers communications effectiveness. McCaffrey explains how to break through defensiveness, and differences of opinion. He describes the art of empathy in the framework of persuasion, motivation and understanding.

The final sessions deal with tension, how to reduce and redirect it. Methods for productively responding to tension are explained and demonstrated. Then McCaffrey tells how to maintain momentum in the daily experiences of life. His last comments are appropriately on fulfillment and the seminar draws to a close.

For many, it was a moving experience, an important weekend. For a few, it was the most important weekend of their lives.

MARKETING VIEWS:
IMPRESS YOUR CLIENT
BY ASKING THE RIGHT QUESTIONS
AT THE RIGHT TIME

By Mike McCaffrey

How would you like to know each time you made a selling presentation that you were the one in control of the meeting? Would you like to have more credibility in such settings? A sense of equality? You can and consistently, if you learn to ask questions well!

This interview process or phase should occupy most of the time you spend face-to-face with a prospective buyer and the buyer should do most of the talking.

One of the most common faults of people who sell is a tendency to avoid doing the necessary work a successful interview requires. Instead, most try to dazzle the potential client with footwork by expounding on all the wonderful things they and their firm have done for others.

Your prospective client/customer really couldn't care less. He needs help and you've got to demonstrate that you're the one who can help him. So the first order of priority is your diagnosis of the client's situation and his needs.

Only when an effective diagnosis is complete can the seller effectively present his strengths. And, not surprisingly, these strengths can perfectly match the potential buyer's needs or wants.

A doctor/patient relationship is an excellent analogy to consider with respect to the interview phase of the selling presentation. The physician spends most of his time examining the patient—taking x-rays, blood pressure and other readings. He also does something very important to his diagnosis. He asks questions. Note how little time a physician spends in writing out the prescription. And he spends no time at all pointing to diplomas or boasting about cures he's affected.

The doctor probes with questions because it is necessary for his diagnosis. Equally as important, he conditions the patient to accept both the diagnosis and the prescription.

Because questions play such an important role in the interview; and because a sale may depend upon how well you ask questions, we will take a close look at this highly learnable skill.

THE VALUE OF QUESTIONING

The single most effective selling tool we have is our ability to ask questions well. People are frequently described as articulate, glib or having the gift of gab. Others say, "That person ought to be a salesman." But glibness is almost totally irrelevant. What really counts is the ability to ask questions effectively.

By asking questions, you acquire a wealth of useful data. You increase your "intelligence information." You show your interest in the buyer, you draw the buyer out and you develop a working relationship. And this is even more important: Questions give you three things, control, credibility and perceived equality.

CONTROL

When you ask a question, you are, in effect, saying who's to talk and what's to talk about. If I ask you, "What do you think of the new Mercedes?" you're not going to talk about the weather. No one else will answer the question. And you're going to speak when I end the question.

If you are concerned about prospective buyers talking too much because you have asked them a question, don't worry. Interrupt and ask another question. "You just said something that triggered a thought in my mind (question)." You maintain control.

CREDIBILITY

Questioning also gives us credibility. The most successful sellers do not need to tout themselves. When they ask incisive, perceptive questions, pretty soon the buyer gets the message: "This guy knows what he's doing. He's thorough. He knows the right questions to ask."

PERCEIVED EQUALITY

Questions also establish a sense of perceived equality. Actually I prefer to control because the greater the control the higher the batting average. While a seller may enter a particular selling situation comfortable in his own knowledge and expertise; he may enter another situation with his "hat in his hand" so to speak—or as an inferior entity. What needs to be established up front is a sense of equality. As a professional in your own field of expertise, you presumably have a vast amount of useful information and data. Further, in most instances you know more about the topic at hand than most people with whom you are speaking.

You are due equal standing with the potential buyer. Give the buyer credit for knowing his/her business, but give yourself credit also for knowing yours.

Reprinted from the April, 1978 issue of *The Executive* of Orange County. Reprinted by permission of Executive Publications, Inc., Newport Beach, Ca.

ASKING TO ASK
(BEFORE YOU ASK)

By asking if you may ask questions of the potential client, you clear the way for an effective interview. You, in effect, get permission to probe. Without that permission you may appear to be "pushy" and in turn find yourself being pushed right out the door.

Approached like that, the prospective client will probably say, "Of course not, go ahead." You will find that people will most often gladly tell you their needs. And all you must do to gain this important knowledge is ask. Specific answers and insight will follow and keep coming as long as you are able to maintain an empathetic attitude.

THE ART OF ASKING QUESTIONS

Armed with the necessary insight into the theory of questioning, you'll find "open end" questions an effective and practical approach to the interview process.

Start with general, open-ended questions which evoke discussion: questions which cannot be answered with a "yes" or "no" or with one word. For example, "What did you think of the world series?" The other person may answer, "Great." To get discussion, ask "What do you think were the two or three really outstanding highlights of the recent world series and why?"

One kind of open-end question—used, for example by IBM sales people—is the best/worst method. They ask "What do you like best about this particular product? Why do you like this, why do you like that? What other things do you like?" Eventually, they'll get around to, "What is it that you don't care for?"

One of the greatest strengths the seller can have going for him is the willingness to walk away from a potential client if he cannot provide a service which meets the eventual need or want. It is not only an ethical necessity, but a marketing asset which gives credibility and authority to what the seller is saying.

However, the willingness to walk away is quite different from spreading out your services like merchandise in a bazaar and, in effect, saying, "Here's what I've got. See anything you need?"

The last point is absolutely central to selling. The objective of the interview is **not** to sell. It is to find out what the prospect needs or wants. If you arrive at that point, you are likely to make the sale. The good seller first seeks to find problems or wants rather than sell solutions.

Appendix D:
Sample Letters

This appendix includes a number of letters, each of which has a specific objective. As you read over the letters, look for specific techniques that you might apply in your business correspondence. Letters are an important part of marketing and selling. How well you are using this medium directly affects your business volume.

SOLICITATION TO NONCLIENT PROSPECTIVE BUYERS

Date

Name of Individual
Title
Company or Organization
Address
City, State, Zip Code

Dear _____:

We met briefly _____ and your name came up again in San Francisco three weeks ago with _____.

I'd like to work for your organization, because I particularly enjoy my work with accountants and feel I know them and their problems well. Enclosed is a brief outline of my services and some references. Please let me know your thoughts on my idea.

Reference 1   Name, title, and company
Address and Phone No.
Reference 2   Name, title, and company
Address and Phone No.
Reference 3   Name, title, and company
Address and Phone No.
Reference 4   Name, title, and company
Address and Phone No.

Sincerely,

Date

Name of Individual
Title
Company or Organization
Address
City, State, Zip Code

Mr. _____:

_____ is a business associate and friend. I have worked for him doing executive development programs for _____. He thought about you and (your company) and felt I might be of service.

Enclosed is some material on myself and my work. After you've had a chance to review this I'd like to call.

Sincerely,

Enclosures: Articles
            Program Information Sheet
            Brochure

Date

Name of Individual
Title
Company or Organization
Address
City, State, Zip Code

Dear _____:

_____, as I am sure you know, has utilized my services for the _____ people in Omaha on three occasions in the last few months.

I conduct seminars on personal development, personal and company goal-setting, communications, decision making and dealing with pressure. In most instances, the spouses have been invited to these programs.

The response has been extremely positive and _____ and his people in Omaha, I am sure, are happy to discuss the benefits derived.

The purpose of this letter is to introduce myself and what I do, and to introduce to you the idea of having a two-day program for your key people in Stamford. This idea was given to me by _____ .

Enclosed is material which further describes my work.

_____ tells me that you will be in Omaha on February 9 and that it is his intention to discuss this idea further with you.

I would like to phone you after you have had an opportunity to review this material and to think about it for a while.

Sincerely,

Enclosures: Brochures
                     Articles

INDIVIDUALS WHO'VE GIVEN THIRD PARTY SUPPORT

Date

Name of Individual
Title
Company or Organization
Address
City, State, Zip Code

Dear _____ :

Your continued support and utilization of my services is very much appreciated.

I am once again impressed with the quality of people that represent _____ .

I hope we can continue to work together in the future.

Best regards,

Information copy to (referral).

_____ a special thanks to you for helping to make this happen again.

Date

Name of Individual
Title
Company or Organization
Address
City, State, Zip Code

Dear _____:

Many thanks for thinking of me regarding referring me to _____.

I appreciate very much your remembering my services throughout the years and hope you continue to benefit from your experience with me.

Best regards,

CONFIRMING PROPOSAL LETTER AFTER WE'VE AGREED IN DISCUSSIONS ON ME AND/OR MY SERVICES

Date

Name of Individual
Title
Company or Organization
Address
City, State, Zip Code

Dear _____:

Nice getting together with you and _____. The following is a proposed agenda for our proposed meeting with the associates:

	Estimated Time
1. Topic	15 Minutes
2. Topic	20 Minutes
3. Topic	10 Minutes
4. Topic	20 Minutes
5. Topic	25 Minutes
6. Topic	25 Minutes
7. Topic	10 Minutes
8. Topic	20 Minutes
9. Topic	20 Minutes
10. Topic	20 Minutes

Hope this meets with your approval. I'll call and let's discuss.

Best Regards,

"KEEPING THE DOOR OPEN"
LETTERS OF SOLICITATION
TO CLIENTS—STAYING
"CLOSE"

Date

Name of Individual
Title
Company or Organization
Address
City, State, Zip Code

Dear _____ :

Happy New Year to you, your family and companies. I have a tentative trip planned to _____ in the next month or two. Here's an idea for your consideration.

Perhaps we could tie in my trip with a day or 1/2 day program follow up for your salespeople—only this program is a different approach to sales. The last program was on sales skills and techniques. This one is on how your people can put to use those skills better.

It concerns itself with what the self-image is, how it influences how we use our sales skills and techniques, how you get it and, most importantly, how you can go about changing and strengthening it so that you can get increasingly comfortable with bigger responsibilities and financial capabilities and, in general, uplifting your psychological and material comfort zone. And people who have higher comfort zones sell more!

I have credibility with your people now and believe I can help them be more effective. The transportation is paid for, the only expense would be a hotel room. Let me know your reaction soon.

Regards,

Date

Name of Individual
Title
Company or Organization
Address
City, State, Zip Code

Dear _____ :

On April 28, I'll be conducting a one-day program in Michigan. I'm writing to ask if it makes any sense for your organization to have me conduct a one-day program on either April 27 or April 29. The travel expense from Southern

California to Michigan is already taken care of, therefore, the expenses to your firm would be minimized.

Some half-day modules for your consideration are:

SELF-IMAGE PSYCHOLOGY—the same program I conducted for the _____ group in Key West January 15, 19___.

COMMUNICATIONS—an enlightening, participative series of exercises designed to emphasize key principles and techniques that lead to better communications.

SELLING PROFESSIONAL SERVICES—you've seen me do half of this (unless we get to role playing case studies—designed by your people—then this becomes a full day).

DEALING WITH PRESSURE AND DECISION MAKING—four ways of handling business and personal pressures. The decision-making session is probably the best one and a half-hour program I present.

I'll call to see if we should talk more.

Best regards,

Date
Name of Individual
Title
Company or Organization
Address
City, State, Zip Code

Dear _____:

Many thanks for asking me to contribute to your meeting at _____. I thoroughly enjoyed it. The people were responsive and appreciative and a speaker always likes that.

I'm glad you, _____, _____ and I had some time to spend together. All in all, it was a most enjoyable and productive time.

I hope I am able to continue working with you and your people on the basis we have in the past. The first program I did was on responsibility and freedom of choice and communications. The second was on self-image psychology (incidentally, I did appreciate your giving me information from the Center for Effective Living—it certainly tells me that you more than understand my thrust).

Enclosed are materials on subjects that are possibilities for another session—one is on marketing of professional services and the other on the selling of professional services. Even though I know your people are very good at these things, some insights on different perspectives usually help.

Thanks again and let me hear from you.

Best regards,

Enclosures: Marketing and Selling Information

PERSONAL NOTE

Date

Dear _____,

Thanks very much for inviting me to speak to your people. I really enjoyed it. They were so inquisitive and responsive I could tell I was making a real contribution.

I appreciate the opportunity.

Best regards,

Date

Name of Individual
Title
Company or Organization
Address
City, State, Zip Code

Dear _____:

Sorry that _____ is not going to offer its key people McCaffrey's FOCUS Seminar right now. I understand there is a form of an austerity program being implemented throughout the divisions with special emphasis on the exclusion of payment for wives. Fair enough. Please understand that I understand. I hope we can do it another time.

Meanwhile, if you have a key man who you want exposed to this experience, I will explain to _____ or _____ how that key man could attend one of my open or public programs this year with no registration fee for his spouse.

Best regards,

Date

Name of Individual
Title
Company or Organization
Address
City, State, Zip Code

Dear _____:

I trust you will do a better job now of screening your _____ friends!

That Friday evening around the pool was one of the highlights of many highlights during a fun and productive weekend, wasn't it? I'm glad we had the chance to meet.

I am also glad to hear of your interest in my work. Enclosed is the information I said I would send regarding the weekend seminar. Although I know it is very quick, perhaps you could send someone to the March 20 program which begins at 8:00 p.m. We only conduct five of these a year.

I hope we can be of service and look forward to working with you.

Best regards,

Enclosures

SOLICITING A CLIENT
WHO IS UNDECIDED

Date

Name of Individual
Title
Company or Organization
Address
City, State, Zip Code

Dear _____:

It was good seeing you again last week. I'm told by _____ that a third party is being contacted regarding the sales training program for your people. You are not yet then sold on M. M.'s ability to do the best job—yet. (repeat)

You are a valued client and I want your work. The fit in terms of my personally relating to your people is good. The fit in terms of my selling situation and their selling situation is almost identical.

This will be a most interacting, involving, back-and-forth, person-to-person selling training session with my experience and their experience being revealed. They will leave with a systematic, effective approach to generating additional business.

Please check my references. I am happy to return to your offices to clarify or amplify any points if you feel that need.

I will do this job well and expect to win this and help make your people more sales productive.

Best regards,

Date

Name of Individual
Title
Company or Organization
Address
City, State, Zip Code

Dear _____ :

It was a pleasure getting to know you this last weekend which was certainly a productive and entertaining one, wasn't it?

Please accept I know your interest in our getting together and talking about a program for your companies. I am looking forward to that meeting but I also want to focus your attention on the husband and wife seminar for _____ and _____. I know this is a quick reaction to our discussion but the reason for this rapid response is that I only conduct the program five times a year and March 20, starting at 8:00 p.m. at Coto de Caza, is the next one.

Enclosed is material regarding the seminar. Perhaps they and you can respond quickly.

Best regards,

Enclosure

Appendix E:
Further Reading:
Bibliographical
Notes

Numerous books have been written on marketing and selling, few are of significant value to the individual professional. In this section, Mike reviews eight such books that he feels have merit and that he recommends in his seminars and workshops.

Fast, Julius M. *Body Language.* New York: M. Evans & Co., Inc., 1970. This book offers good insights into various nonverbal communications. This is an easy-to-read book dealing with what various body positions mean, how they influence others, and how they interact with the spoken word. As the author points out, these are only indications, but are generally reliable. Reading the buyer is of utmost importance, so this information can prove extremely useful to the seller.

Karras, Chester L. *The Negotiating Game: How to Get What You Want.* New York: Thomas Y. Crowell Co., 1970. This is an excellent book by one of the outstanding negotiating and training people in the country. He uses various psychological strategies for gaining advantage, uncovers hidden assumptions and motivation factors, and points out styles, tools, tactics, and bargaining levers. The reason I like this book is because it parallels my thinking with the need to combine attitudes and techniques. His line, "Individuals who have a good self-image initiate attempts to influence, tend to reject influence from others, and believe they are more influential than others who see themselves in a lesser light," demonstrates the parallel in thinking.

Malloy, John. *Dress for Success*. New York: Random House, 1975. This is a very engaging book because Malloy bases his conclusions on experiments rather than on fashion or fads. It is a semi-scientific approach to which clothes are "right for the situation." Malloy's main theme is "dress toward the conservative, business side." If you do, you'll win more often. Some exceptions are allowed for in certain parts of the country. Malloy is an Easterner. This book was sequelled by a book on dress for career women.

Mandino, Og. *The Greatest Salesman in the World*. New York: Frederick Fell, 1968. If you want to be inspired and feel good about selling and marketing, read this one. This is a biblical-like story about a young boy who wants to become successful and attain all that goes with success, and of an old man who shows him how to accomplish this through selling. It is a skillfully told story with a rich message.

Nierenberg, Gerald I. and Calero, Henry H. *How to Read a Person Like a Book*. New York: Hawthorn Books, Inc. 1971. This book is filled with graphic illustrations about what various body positions mean. Nierenberg is the author of a book called, *The Art of Negotiation*. Gestures that indicate openness, defensiveness, readiness, confidence, boredom, expectancy, suspicion, and so on are described and pictured. Understanding the environment in which these gestures take place is also considered. This is a book worth reading even if only to get a few clues that will help in selling.

Ringer, Robert. *Winning through Intimidation*. Los Angeles: Los Angeles Book Publishing Co., 1974. Robert Ringer is brassy, brash, and more aggressive than any professional person I've seen, or hope to see. But his selling principles are sound. His experience is primarily in real estate, emphasizing big deals. He uses intimidation as his main weapon. Scare or bluff the buyer into a weaker position than yours. While Ringer emphasizes selling, he is an outstanding marketer also.

Shook, Robert. *Winning Images*. New York: Pocket Books, 1978. This is not a sophisticated book for sophisticated professionals, but it deals with public imagery. One of the key marketing concepts is that people are attracted to perceived value. This book is primarily concerned with impressions, appearances, perceptions for the single practitioner, or for the small firm approach. Since I fit into that size category I can appreciate what this book presents.

Wilson, Aubrey. *The Marketing of Professional Services.* New York: McGraw-Hill, 1972. A thorough, academic approach to marketing with an emphasis on buyer/client needs. Wilson is English, and his background and experience appears to be primarily from a practice in England. The book is stronger in marketing with special emphasis on research and planning. Selling is not as highlighted, and ethical constraints on selling and marketing are considered more from a British viewpoint from the perspective of the previous decade.

Index